So…What's Next?

by

Amyre Makupson

authorHOUSE

1663 Liberty Drive, Suite 200
Bloomington, Indiana 47403
(800) 839-8640
www.authorhouse.com

First published by AuthorHouse 07/27/05

ISBN: 1-4184-4139-2 (Paperback)
ISBN: 1-4184-4140-6 (Dust Jacket)

Printed in the United States of America
Bloomington, Indiana

This book is printed on acid-free paper.

DEDICATION

To my mother, father and brother. To my sisters, husband and children. To all of the beautiful people in my life, past and present…for your love, support and encouragement.

TABLE OF CONTENTS

PROLOGUE

Obsessed might be too strong of a word but I have certainly been fascinated with the hereafter for a long time. I think about it a lot. It all started the first time someone I loved died. It was a life-altering event. I was 19 at the time. Of all of the things that have happened in my life since that time including other deaths, marriage, children, illnesses, career, even murder…all kinds of forms of happiness and sadness, peaks and valleys, it is still the event of my life. I'll tell you much more about that later.

Perhaps another reason for my fascination is my career. I was in the television news business for 25 years. I was a news anchor and talk show host all of those 25 years. Because of my business, I was quite often asked to speak at funerals for relatives and friends. I don't mean read a passage. I mean speak! People assume that because one can talk on television, he or she can talk anywhere. I had never in my wildest imagination ever thought I would speak at a funeral much less some 25 of them. A strange thing happened over time though. I used to dread it. Later, I came to feel very comfortable with it and even honored by it. It became a way to share ones innermost thoughts on the life of someone who meant so much.

All of that funeral speaking leaves its mark. I began to wonder about *what's next?* I would find myself looking and thinking and imagining. I came to the conclusion that the person in the box, the *life* in the box was in no way over. You don't just put bodies in boxes and call their lives over. That's not reasonable. Funerals remember the end of a dimension. They don't represent the end of existence. We are just not capable of understanding the other levels of life.

So I continually thought about *what's next?* I began to wonder about my father and mother and brother. I wondered what they might be doing. I thought just because they can't move anymore, doesn't mean they don't exist anymore. And then came the big question, what will I be doing after I leave this earth? They are thoughts that enter my mind often. They are also thoughts that beg many questions and have no absolute answers.

Death is strange. It brings about a spread of possibly every emotion known to man and woman. I believe it brings out the worst in all of us. Why? Because it hurts so badly and there is nothing, absolutely nothing you can do about it. Let me start out by saying that I have had absolutely no formal education or training in death and dying. But I have had real life education. I have lost people I love. That truly is an education. The difference is, you are your own teacher.

We all know that death brings about great sorrow. Depending on the circumstances, it brings joy. It is very painful to see someone you love suffer and know there is nothing that can be done for them. It is very painful to watch someone you love lie in a state where there is no dignity, no quality. It is even worse to watch someone lie in pain and know there is no hope that anything will ever get any better. There is no hope that one day that person will sit up and smile or have a conversation with you. So it is easy to understand how death might bring about relief, if not joy.

Death also brings with it shock and disbelief. It scares you. It brings about anxiety and pain and suffering. It even brings about anger. That kind of surprised me when I realized it. I realized that you can be angry at whatever or whoever because someone you love has been taken away from you. But you can also get angry with the person who died, as if he or she had something to do with it, as if he or she could have prevented it. " I told him not to drink at parties." " I told her not to take that flight." " Why couldn't she have just jumped out of the way of that car?" "Couldn't he have left the office just a few minutes later and avoided that accident?" The "what ifs" are mind-boggling!

Still, death is death. It's a very emotional experience. We think with our hearts instead of our minds. We learn the true definition of finality. This is something you can do nothing about no matter who you are, no matter how much money you have, no matter what religion you practice or where you live.

Death also makes us feel guilty. The hardest person to really forgive is oneself. You think about the lie you told. You think about the unnecessary trouble you caused. You remember the times you could have been nicer, more patient, more sensitive. You think about all of the things you could have done, the things that would have taken so little and meant so much and you just feel so helplessly guilty. And bottom line, there is nothing you can do about it.

In researching this venture, I found that everyone has thoughts on death and what might be waiting for them. Most people don't talk about it in general conversation because they are afraid others will think they're strange. But we all have thoughts. And I was surprised to discover that when asked, almost everyone was willing and even eager to express their feelings. These thoughts are formed by life experiences. They come from religious beliefs. They come from sensations and presences felt. They come from dreams and stories told. They guide our lives in some ways. Certainly, they give us thoughts, hopes and beliefs about what happens next.

The bottom line is …when you're gone, you're gone! Or, are you? We all think different things and for different reasons. This book is a compilation of ordinary peoples' thoughts, people who have had no formal education in death and dying, and what they think happens next…and why!

TRY TO FIGURE!!

We spend the early part of our lives simply living it…getting used to it, exploring it and, if we're lucky, enjoying it. We contemplate today and the day after wondering what we might do and what might happen. We are carefree and young and hopeful. And that is exactly as it should be. But as we get older, we begin to realize that life is not forever and we begin to consciously deal with our own mortality. That's scary.

As a child, you believe you will live forever. I don't think it occurs to the average child that he or she might get sick beyond the common cold or stomachache. The thought of cancer or multiple sclerosis or muscular dystrophy or heart disease does not enter the mind of the average child. And for those of us who are blessed with worry free childhoods…for those of us who have yet to lose someone, leaving this world is not even a conscious thought. Not now anyway. It's only as life toughens that our thoughts begin to even formulate and then change.

It's a different story by the time you hit your teens and 20s. We begin to have thoughts about what might be next. And many times those thoughts are formed by religious influences. They are also influenced by conversation with friends and family and probably for most of us, fortunately, they are more pleasant than not. But as we come into ourselves and we start to *really* grow up and feel the harsh realities of life, start to lose people we love, we begin to put some serious thought into "next". Am I going to be able to talk with my parents? Can I see my brother again? Can we relive the days that we remember as so happy? Does it start all over again? What age will I be? Will I be in the first grade or will I be the parent of a first grader? Will my parents play with my kids or are they still playing with me? WHOA!

This age thing is really something when you think in terms of the hereafter. If I go to heaven and I'm the age I am *now,* how old are my parents? They passed away a long time ago but in my personal scheme of things, are we still on the same level? This time frame thing is really confusing. How am I going to be with my parents when maybe they wanted to be with *their* parents? Can they be with theirs and I tag along? You may not have even been born when your parents' parents were alive. How will *my* kids fit in? At what stage will parents and grandparents be when they meet their future generations...who are now past? Confusing? You bet! Thoroughly! Somehow the time thing has to be transcended. It simply will not work any other way, at least we can't figure it out in any reasonable, acceptable manner. We don't know any other dimension. We only know what we live. And because we don't know another dimension, some of us believe, or at least hope the afterlife continues in the very dimension in which we lived on earth. Maybe that is exactly what we want to think...all happy times, of course.

We try to answer those questions in ways we can accept them. Most of us believe, or at least we convince ourselves that we will join those who have died before us. We *will* see those who meant and mean so much. We *will* have a chance to be together again. That absolutely *has* to be, doesn't it? Sure, it does! But sometimes panic sets in. What if this is it? What if when someone dies, they *really* die. Like, that's it. You won't see them again or talk to them again under any circumstance, on any level, at any time. But it cannot be. That doesn't make any sense. That would be ridiculous. There has to be purpose. There has to be more to life than the peaks and valleys we experience on this earth. Why would there be generations of people who simply live and learn and do things and die? Are some people born to be smart and invent things like the air conditioner only so that future generations can be cool? Of course not. That doesn't make any sense. But who says it has to? For people who believe, that's where faith comes in. What is faith? It is substance of things believed...evidence of things unseen.

This death thing is strange really. Very peculiar! Even though we may have dealt with death in so many ways...having lost people we know...having lost people we love...feeling badly because someone famous died who we never personally knew but admired from afar...we have seen and experienced it time and time again. But somehow, we convince ourselves that it doesn't apply to us. Somehow, I am going to be the first one who lives forever. I mean, how could the sun possibly shine if I'm not here to see it? The world couldn't go on without me. Even though we know that is not possibly true...we can somehow convince ourselves it might be. Is it not a little difficult to imagine a world without you?

It is very difficult to deal with one's own death. When you stop to think about the fact that you can see, feel, touch, hear, laugh, cry, think, reason, you can begin to feel overwhelmed. How could tomorrow begin if I die today? That just can't happen, can it? Sure it can. But that thought, that reality somehow is just too much to consciously deal with. It's back burner all the way. And it's probably a good thing that it is back burner. Can you imagine what a gloom and doom place this would be if everyone was running around worrying about dying? I mean *really* worrying about dying. What an awful thought. No one would ever be able to get a thing done, much less smile again.

So...What's Next?

Let's back up all the way to the beginning...*before* the beginning. Where were we before we were born? What was I doing? Is that what it's going to be like *after* I die? Do we go back into that abyss where we won't be able to remember what happened? Maybe we can only recognize and be cognizant of right now. Lots of questions. Just as many answers. It depends, of course, on who you ask.

WHAT IS THIS DÉJÀ VU STUFF?

It has happened to me. It certainly gets your attention. It startles you. Not in a scary sort of way but in a way that makes you think. It seems to come out of nowhere. But when it hits, it hits. And it sticks! You try to figure it out. Sometimes you can but sometimes it makes no sense at all. So we just let it go.

Sometimes it's a smell. Sometimes it is an expression or an act. Sometimes it seems like a recollection. You're someplace…someplace you know you have never been before. But all of a sudden, everything is just too familiar. You get the sense that you've been there before…the exact same place, under the exact same circumstance. But you *know* you have not. It doesn't make any sense but at the same time, it makes all the sense in the world. Like a story a friend shared with me. It just blew me away. It was fascinating.

My friend Gwen grew up in the city of Detroit. Her family was poor. They had a lot of kids and not a lot of money. One day in grade school, the teacher talked about maple syrup. She asked the kids if anyone knew how maple syrup was made. One of the kids raised her hand and offered an explanation. She explained the process as she understood it. Out of nowhere, Gwen raised her hand in protest. She said "No. That's wrong." Then Gwen began a very detailed explanation of exactly how maple syrup is made. Maple is in a tree. If you wanted to get it out, you had to drive a nail-like object in the tree, put some sort of container under the hole and maple would drip into the container. Then you take it, refine it, process it and all the rest. Her explanation was much more involved than that but she gave a perfect account and description as to how maple syrup is made. The very surprised teacher praised Gwen for giving such a detailed and accurate description.

As Gwen sat down she all of a sudden realized that she didn't have any idea as to why she knew how maple syrup is made. She never studied it. She didn't know anything about maple syrup and didn't even like it. She had never visited a place where maple syrup was made. She had never been out of the city of Detroit much less to a, in her words, a maple growing state. She was absolutely stunned at herself and couldn't figure out why she said what she said, where her information came from and maybe more importantly, how she even got the nerve to get up and talk. To this very day she doesn't understand it. Gwen is about 50 years old now. She was absolutely shocked. She still talks about it! The maple *mystery* happened in the third grade.

That's not exactly deja-vu in the sense that we think of it. It's not like she was recounting a story from work as a maple syrup maker. But where *did* it come from? This is a poor kid from Detroit who had never left her neighborhood much less traveled to another state. Had she seen a movie and maybe forgotten about it? Remember, she was only in the third grade. Did she use to work for some kind of a syrup making company and suddenly found herself in a past lifetime perhaps with the teacher hitting exactly on the focus of a former life? Did she ever dream of maple syrup, forget the dream but somehow instantly recall it knowing the information was useful? There are probably tons of different scenarios. We have to draw our own conclusions.

Why is this story even in here? There is at least a suggestion that life after life, brings on another life. Some people think we keep doing it until we get it right. Maybe we do have different lives and somehow all of our past lives go into our present one and contribute. Maybe every second we have ever lived goes into the second we are living right now. Maybe we move to different environments, live with different people, have different experiences and somehow, at some point, there are cross roads and connections and it comes together if only in moments.

I have smelled things before. I have heard things before. I have had sensations before that take me into deep thought. It's difficult to explain. But these sensations connect me with memories that are sometimes so faded and soft, I can't really give you an accurate description. They just take me somewhere I know I have been before, but somewhere I can't consciously explain to you now. And, thank God, it is always a pleasant experience.

So the question is…how does déjà vu, something that is in the past, get connected to now? How can we be carried back to something that we can't consciously recollect yet something that feels so in the present? Is today part of yesterday and tomorrow? What did I tell you? Many more questions than answers!

NOT AFRAID TO DIE!

What do I think? I think a lot of things. My thoughts have changed over the years. They have been influenced by many things. Life experiences make you change your mind all the time. Everything we think is based on what happens in our lives. That doesn't change. Every day brings new experiences upon which to base our thoughts and beliefs. It doesn't matter how old you are. It's just that the older you get, the more experiences you have. I do think sometimes though, that it's better to be a child. Your experiences are fewer. Your thoughts are simpler. Life is more fun…you just don't realize it at the time. Children have great fantasies. Anything is possible. In fact, everything is possible and exactly as you want it. Just because it is. That can be a blessing, maybe especially at the time of death.

Adulthood takes away a lot of fantasy but it also give you thought processes to help make sense of life. If your ideas truly make sense *to you,* then that's your reality. You become comfortable with your thoughts. You can relax and believe at least to the extent that you can, that you have figured it out. Or at least we can live with what we have "figured" out. What is that expression again? Faith is substance of things believed…evidence of things unseen.

I don't know what happens after death. No one does. But I know what I *think* happens and what I would *like* to happen. So does everyone else. Everyone thinks about this topic but not everyone talks about it. We tend to just keep our thoughts to ourselves. But, believe me, it doesn't take much prompting to get others to share their thoughts. Once asked, most were extremely eager. Some difficult to stop!

My thoughts, like everyone else's, are based on my life experiences. This is the one that lies at the base of my opinion. My brother died many years ago. He was in a motorcycle accident. Actually, he was behind a friend's house where he and others were showing off and doing "tricks" on the bike. He was not really familiar or experienced at all on motorcycles. In fact, the motorcycle wasn't even his. It belonged to someone else and he was just borrowing it for a day or so. At any rate, it was way too powerful for him. As he darted down the alley trying to raise the front wheel of the cycle, my brother lost control and struck a light pole. Unfortunately, it's more accurate to say his head struck a light pole. He died a very short time later in the hospital.

We only lived a couple of blocks away. Although it was some 35 years ago, I still remember everything as if it happened only last week. I remember the phone call. I was in the kitchen. I answered it. My mother was cooking hamburgers. In fact, let me back up a minute. As my mother was cooking, Rudy came into the kitchen. He said he was running to his friend's house for a minute. My mother asked him not to be long because dinner was almost ready. Rudy said, "Don't worry, Mom. I'll be back before they're done." That is *exactly* what he said. "I'll be back before they're done." I can still hear him saying it.

Back to the phone call. I answered it and heard a neighbor say, "There's been an accident. Come down here right away." I said nothing. My mother looked at me. She knew something was drastically wrong. We ran out of the kitchen and drove down the street. The trip probably took us about 2 minutes...if that. My brother was lying in the alley making a moaning/gurgling sound. He had no helmet on. There was blood. The bike was mangled.

Somehow everyone else arrived. My father was a physician. I remember him touching my brother's forehead. "His skull is broken." It's strange the things you think. Although I knew he would never make it, I remember thinking right at that point, about spending the rest of the summer visiting him in the hospital bringing him gifts. I think I was trying to convince myself that this was going to end up positively. We didn't wait for the ambulance. We had a station wagon. We drove him to the hospital. Rudy died there.

The first stage of my grief was disbelief. I simply could not believe it. I kept replaying the events going to the scene of the accident. I kept replaying the conversation on the telephone. I remember the ride to the hospital. I remember waiting in the emergency room. I remember a lot of people around...family and friends. I remember the doctor coming in and telling us he was dead. I remember numbness. I remember what I had on...khaki jeans and a navy blue tee shirt. I remember the blood on my pants because I held Rudy's head as he lay in the alley. I remember my mother and father holding each other in the waiting room. I remember my sisters and everyone crying in the emergency room. I actually remember thinking that he would be admitted to the hospital and that I would visit every day, all day and bring him all kinds of things while he was there. I don't remember accepting that he was dead.

My bedroom where we lived was in the back of the house. We had a pretty good sized backyard and a garage on the far side of the yard. We had lived in that house for maybe 15 years at the time. It was a corner house and the garage let out on to the side street. So you would enter the garage from the street and not from the yard. There was a sewer cover at the base of the driveway. In order to get into the garage, you would drive over the cover. It made a funny sort of a sound...the very heavy sound of a large metal cover sort of "slapping" on concrete. It was loud. It was definitive. It was a sound that I laid there in that bed and heard over and over again for some 15 years. My father would come home from work late in the evening. So many nights, as he drove in the garage, I heard his car as it ran over the sewer cover. I could pick that specific sound out of a thousand.

Our garage door was hard to close. You had to slam it...really *slam* it. I heard that slam also a thousand times, probably several thousand. As I lay in bed that night after Rudy died, reliving every second since 6:00pm, on Saturday, July 22, 1967...I specifically heard the sewer cover make its sound. About 10 seconds later, I heard the garage door slam and about 5 seconds later, I hear my brother call my name. "Amyre", he said. I was so frightened I ran out of the room and jumped in my parents' bed. It was so new. It was so strange. I was absolutely scared to death. I was terrified.

When I told my parents what had just happened, they just sort of looked at me. Their grief, needless to say, was almost insurmountable. Everyone says losing a child is the worst thing that can happen to anyone in life. Probably not too many parents would disagree with that. They listened. They comforted me. And then my mother said that if that ever happened again, and I was frightened, don't run. Send him to her.

I believe with all my heart, Rudy was there. Some might say I imagined it and make a good case that I did. But I believe he was there. I believe he was going to tell me that everything was OK. I believe he wanted to comfort me and everyone else through me. I will never, never forgive myself for running. To this day, I can't believe I did that. I have always wished he would come back. I have looked for him every single day since that day. I want him to know I'm ready now. I want him to know that I will not run.

Another strange twist to this happening is that on the very same night, a very short time later according to the account of a girlfriend of mine, Rudy came to her in a dream. She was a childhood friend with whom we played often. She and I are still dear friends today. In her dream, she was in the living room of her house and looked out the window. Rudy was there. He told her that he just came to say that everything is all right. I think since he couldn't give me that message, he gave it to Barbara.

This is something else that I witnessed that makes me believe there is *something* after this life. My mother was Creole. Her heritage was a mixture of French, Spanish and African American. When she and her siblings were school-aged children in New Orleans, actually St. John's Parish, they spoke French in the home. Actually, her grandparents, who lived with them, pretty much spoke only French. Their English was broken. Anyway, my mother and her siblings, especially her sister, were very fluent in French. One sister was so fluent, that she would actually stay after school and teach their teachers correct French pronunciation, grammar and other things. As they grew older, married and moved way from New Orleans, some of their family kept up their French, especially my Aunt Isaure. But most of them seldom spoke it other than a sentence or two here and there. For my mother, French became almost non-existent.

My grandmother, my mother's mother, died relatively young. My mother was barely a teenager at the time. My mother seldom spoke of her mother. Every now and then, we'd hear stories. If you asked, my mother would always answer questions but she seldom brought up such a conversation. She just didn't talk about her much – for whatever reason.

My mother, Amyre, had the very unfortunate fate of getting Alzheimer's disease. That's a neurological disorder that severely affects the brain. It's a very long, slow, devastating process that robs you of your memory. It robs you of your life because you can't remember much of anything or anyone – including your spouse, children, basic things in life like what a toothbrush or bathtub is for. That's a very watered down description but it's accurate. Anyway, the day before my mother's death, as she lay in her hospital bed, withering away, unconscious, trying her best, I guess, to not slip away, she began to talk to her mother *in French!* I don't know what she was saying, but it was obvious she was having a conversation with her mother and she was having it in French! Now remember, my mother barely if ever spoke French. I'm sure she forgot most of it. And she never spoke of her mother. I was absolutely dumbfounded. My dying mother was talking with her mother who had died some 50 years ago. I *know* my grandmother was comforting her daughter and trying to help her with her transition. I could never put into words the sense of comfort it gives me to have reason to believe my grandmother made it easier for my mother and that my mother will make it easier for me. This experience has made me *not afraid to die!*

I don't dream much about my mother, or father or brother. Unfortunately, when I do, not all of the time but most of the time, the dreams are unpleasant. That really disturbs me. I wish I knew why. The only thing I can think about is the fact that my brother died so unnecessarily, so young. The last years of my mother's life were so sad. Alzheimer's disease is so heartbreaking. It's almost unbearable. My father's death was a horror. I'll tell you a little bit about it.

My dad was murdered in our home. Some young person broke in in an attempted robbery and shot him to death. It's a very long story with a lot of intricacies but the short of it is that someone came in looking to take money. They left taking a life and forever changed the lives of so many others.

My father was a man's man. He ruled his house. He was flamboyant. He was very handsome and very smart. In fact to this day, he is still the youngest person ever to have graduated (1940s) from Meharry Medical College in Nashville, Tennessee. He was a fun person, very family oriented, loving and a very good provider. We took family vacations, went out a lot and entertained a lot. We had parties all the time. He loved kids. But make no mistake, he was also the boss. If he said do something, you did it. I'm not trying to make him sound mean. My childhood was fabulous but you did what he said. That's just the way it was. I don't ever remember asking many questions. I just did what I was told. I loved him very much but he almost always had the last word. That was the rule. At least that's the way I remember it.

On August 29, 1975, I had plans to go out. Actually, I was going to spend the night with my fiancé. I would never, ever have said that to him. I wouldn't admit it to this day. So I made up some sort of a story about going to Dayton, Ohio, my fiancé's hometown. I told my father my fiancé's family was planning a party for me and I wanted to be there to help. He told me that he didn't want me to go. In fact, he told me to stay home. He said he had something important he wanted me to do. He said it was important that I be home. Well, no matter what, I had made up my mind that I was leaving, regardless of what plans he might have. I left. That was the first time in my life I ever knowingly went against his specific wishes. It was the very first time I said "no". I had simply decided I was too old to not do something I

15

wanted to do. It was the very first time in my life I specifically defied his wishes. Understand that was a very big deal. We did not say no to our father.

That was the very night the intruder came in our house and shot him to death. He and my mother were home. I was supposed to be there too. My room was at the top of the front stairs. I would have been the first person the intruder saw. Maybe the first person he shot. I think about that every single day of my life. The first time I defied my father's wishes and said "no" probably saved my life. I just can't express what a major happening that was for me to have said "no" when I knew he was opposed. It just didn't happen like that in my house. But somebody or something got me out of there. Luck? Fate? Destiny? Who knows? Who ever will?

So what do I know? I guess I don't *know* anything. But I definitely believe there is more to life than living on this earth. There is something. There is a connection. There will be peace and togetherness. I will see my brother and mother and father and a lot of other precious friends and relatives whom I miss so much. And almost everyone else I have talked with believes there is much more to come as well. When will we know this? Some say they know it already. When can we prove this? Not until we die. But what follows are thoughts and reasons why so many people believe as they do.

STEPH

My mother passed away during the month of September. She had a long and hard illness. It was probably about 2 months after she died when I had what I can only call a visit. It was in the middle of the afternoon. I had just made myself a salad for lunch. While I was sitting in the kitchen preparing to eat it, I saw my mother walk from the family room into my kitchen. My mother was 74 years old when she died and she had been ill for a while. But when I saw her, when she came into my kitchen, she looked as though she was in her 50s. She had on clothes that she would have worn to work. She had been a secretary. But the point is, she looked very healthy and very young.

My mother told me that I was not taking proper care of myself. She said salads were fine but that I should really be eating better. We actually had a conversation. I defended my eating habits. She said my lunch was fine but she also repeated that I should be taking better care of myself in general. I looked down at my plate. When I looked up again, she was gone.

I was certainly surprised but I was not scared. We were having a conversation that we would normally have had. It was very nice. I was not at all afraid because she looked so good to me. Remember, she had been ill and failing at the time of her death. This was so special. She looked so good. I had not been sleeping. I was fully awake. I had been doing things around the house. It was not a dream. It was beautiful.

After she left, I just sat there. I thought, what did I just see? Was she really here? Was I dreaming? Absolutely not! I did not understand what was going on other than she came to give me a message. She also came to tell me that she was fine and pleased with where she is. I believe it was a confirmation that I should not worry because she is fine.

I truly believe there is a spirit and there is life after death. We are not put here on this earth just to exist and then stop existing. I think we will all have to account for the things that we do here on earth that are hurtful in any way. Still though, I do struggle with the concept of life after death a lot. I am Catholic so that is my base but I struggle with some of the concepts of the church. My church used to teach that babies who were not baptized babies go to a place called limbo. That doesn't make any sense. A baby can't pay for things over which he or she had no control.

Theories and teachings just have to make sense. I believe there is an afterlife. We talk about things today and question things because we have the opportunity to read and to think and to see alternatives. Faith is a gift but it is hard to accept everything by total faith. That may have been easier centuries ago but today is different. I don't think a lack of total faith makes one a bad person. If something doesn't make sense, I struggle with it.

I am not a sensitive person when you speak of other dimensions but my mother's visit was so real to me. I remember feeling puzzled. I remember thinking "how is she here"? But she was here. That's really all I can say.

I am not ashamed or embarrassed by my experience. I am only amazed that it happened to me. Maybe I should be more spiritual. There is definitely something beyond this world. I'm not in a hurry to find out even though I know I will at some point. I know there is some sort of peacefulness and happiness. My mother was so calm. She just sat down and talked to me. It was beautiful! I just wish she hadn't left so soon.

GINGER

I have had two events happen in my life that have helped to shape what I think about life after death. The first one happened when I was 16. That was some 35 years ago. But I will tell you about the second one first. It was an experience like no other. I was in bed. It was so real to me that I actually got out of bed and wrote down every single detail so that I would not forget a single thing.

It happened about six months after my mother passed away. At the time, I was working the late shift at a television station. I got home about 4 in the morning. I went to bed but I got up early because I had to take my son to school. I took him, came back home, got back in bed and fell asleep.

As I dozed off, I started hearing noises down the hallway. Even though I knew there was no one else in the house, the noises alarmed me. Then I remembered that I had left the door unlocked so I began to get concerned. I opened my eyes and saw the dog come walking in to the room. I felt better right away…or at least a little more relaxed. I thought the noise was Sidney in his metal crate. WHEW!

I closed my eyes again but for some reason, I had an impression in my mind of a "buzz" of friendly voices. It was sort of like when you're in a room full of relatives or friends and everybody's talking and enjoying each other…like a holiday dinner gathering. Then, all of a sudden, I heard my moms voice saying, "Ginger". At that exact moment, all of the other voices went away. The only thing I can equate it to is that it was like she was coming from somewhere. She was sort of like popping through to me. The mental scene was friendly voices. There is really no visual to tell you about. I simply heard friendly, happy voices making sounds. I did not hear conversations. I heard friendly voices talking but I could not distinguish any words other than my mother calling to me.

My eyes were closed. I opened them. I recognized that I was in my bedroom. I saw the dog. I closed my eyes again. Then, I said, "Mom?" I heard her voice say "I'm here." It was a very cool thing. (Ginger began to weep as she continued her story) I opened my eyes again. I closed them again and I forced myself to say out loud, "I hear you." I wanted her to know that I knew she was there. I didn't just respond in my head. I said out loud, "I hear you."

The next thing I know, I felt like she was lying down beside me. But the funny thing was, I was lying on the edge of the bed and she was lying beside me on the side where there was no more bed. She would have to have been lying on air. There was no visual but I could feel her next to me. I could not feel her touch me with her hands or her fingers but I could feel that she was there...lying on air because there was no more bed. I felt her body next to mine. It's hard for me to explain because I had never experienced anything like that before. I felt her touch...but I could not feel her touch me. I felt like maybe you would feel when a heat lamp comes on. I felt suddenly warmed. I felt like I was enveloped by a wave of pure love and joy and happiness...like there was absolutely nothing wrong with where she was. I felt glorious.

As I say this aloud, I realize there are no words to describe what I am trying to tell you. I think I got a physical feel of heaven. I think I felt rapture. I remember thinking this must be what heaven feels like. My mom was visiting me. I could feel her presence, her body and her soul. Inside myself, I could feel something that was truly amazing. I don't know the words to describe it. I felt love! I felt all was right with the world. I felt pure joy and absolute goodness.

I opened my eyes and the feeling immediately went away. My dog was still there but my mother wasn't. I closed my eyes again really quickly, trying to keep the feeling but I couldn't. It was over. So I just laid there and then I went back to sleep. It was not a dream. It was a visitation. I cannot explain how I feel now or how I felt at the moment I felt her touch. All I know is if that's what heaven is like, it is going to be fabulous. I don't think there are physical places like heaven is here and hell is over there. But if the next place is what I felt, I cannot wait!

My first experience happened around Christmas time. Everyone in my house was asleep in bed. I was the only one who was awake. I was downstairs lying on the couch, taking in the mood, looking at the Christmas lights on our tree and just enjoying the feel, the look and the smell of the season. We had a fresh tree with strings and strings of lights on it. Those trees are beautiful. They were worrisome though. Way too often, you would hear news stories about houses burning to the ground and entire families being wiped out because everyone went to bed and left the Christmas tree lights on

I'm not sure but perhaps I had dozed off. Anyway, all of a sudden, I heard a voice in my head saying, "Wake up". It was a pleasant voice. Not loud. Not intimidating, just a voice telling me to wake up. It seemed to do just that – wake me up. I immediately did and thought, "Whose voice was that? Who was that?" For some reason, I started thinking about my Aunt Rosie. She popped right in my mind. She was my favorite aunt. She had recently passed away. I loved her and I missed her. I wanted the voice to be hers. The funny thing is, I must have known it was something a little different because my next thought was, "That's my grandma Yates". For some reason, I knew it was my grandma. I also immediately knew she had awakened me to turn the Christmas lights off. She never said anything else but that was the message I got. It was instantaneous. I had the feeling there would have been a fire if I had not gotten up and turned off the lights.

Now, here's the really strange thing. I mentioned this to my Dad the next morning. I tried to explain exactly what happened. He didn't like talk like this. He was uncomfortable with anything strange or suspicious or supernatural. He was a complete skeptic. But his face looked different…a little strange. Something hit a cord with him. I asked him what was wrong. He began telling me that he had had a vision of his mother standing at the foot of his bed last night, the very same night I heard the voice. She did not say anything to him. She was just there. My dad didn't really go into any details when he told me about it. He never even said if he opened his eyes or not. He just said she was there…standing at the foot of his bed. He called it a vision but he didn't say if it was a mental vision or a physical vision. Whatever it was, it clearly bothered him. He was convinced he had seen his mother.

I think my grandma saved our lives that night. I think that's why she came to me and to her son (my dad) because there were lights on the tree and a fire could have easily started. She probably did double duty…visiting him and me to make sure somebody got the message. We didn't actually compare times but it was the same night and we both woke up with the story still fresh in our minds.

The experience didn't scare me at all. In fact, it was very comforting even though I was downstairs by myself. I have a few aunts who are really open to this kind of thing so I used to hear talk of it all the time. In fact, it used to scare me. I used to say out loud, "Please don't visit me. Please don't visit me." So for this to happen, it is surprising that I accepted it so calmly and openly. I just knew somehow this experience was different and nothing to be afraid of. It was not a normal dream. Sometimes you have dreams that seem real but somehow, you know they're not. I don't know how to describe it other than the fact that the voice was just right there in my head. It was real. It was so different from any other dream. There is just no mistaking that it was something other than real.

These two incidents make me wonder why it is that some people can come back and others can't. I don't think we can control that. If we could, everyone would come back to touch people who have been left behind. There is so much more going on than we can think and feel. We just don't know how to intellectualize it. It makes me less afraid to die. I still don't want to die right now but I will not be afraid when it happens. That's what these experiences taught me. Don't be afraid to die.

We all need something spiritual. How we come to that is up to us individually. I don't think there is a god who takes care of us and who watches over us. Too many bad things happen in the world for that to be. But I definitely believe there is more than meets the eye. Just because we can't see it, touch it, feel it, taste it…doesn't mean it's not there.

ANGELA

I would feel guilty if I died at this point in my life because I would leave so much that would have to be cleaned up. I would feel guilty if someone else had to clean up all of my junk. Wouldn't you hate to have to clean up someone else's junk?

The realization about death has always been with me and my family. It may have something to do with the fact that my uncle was in the funeral business. We went to the funeral home all of the time…sometimes every day. We were always around death or dead bodies. It was no big deal. Because of that, we had a comfort level with at least the presence of death.

The first realization of death comes with the death of the first loved one to die. It could be a grandparent. It could be a schoolmate. Death comes with questions. What happens in that scenario? What is the ritual that we go through? What do we do? What is expected of us? Everybody grieves and goes through some kind of ritual. My question might be: "Where did they go"?

I have felt the very strong presence of someone who died. In fact, I know I have been in the presence of someone who died. It was my brother-in law. He came to me in a very physical kind of way. The funny thing is, I thought it was my grandmother because she had passed away earlier that very same day. Let me try to explain it.

I worked for my brother-in-law. He was a physician. I was with him in his office from 10:00 in the morning until 7:00 in the evening for many years. One day, while I was at work, I got notice that my grandmother had died. So Tom, my brother-in-law, went to see about her and my family and try to help in any way he could. Later that evening, when I went home, I was absolutely exhausted. I got ready to go to bed. I have to tell you, I am very particular about my sheets. They have to be folded in a very specific way. I folded them exactly the way I like them and I was about to turn out the light and all of a sudden, I turned to the door and felt this wave go through my body. Something happened from the very bottom of my feet. It was like an electric wave or shock that started at my feet and went all the way up my entire body. It actually caused me to shiver. The very first thing that came to my mind was that it was a visit from my grandmother.

The thought made me a little panicky but the next thought that came into my mind was, "She's my grandmother. She would never hurt me." I calmed down, turned the light off and got into bed. The presence left and I fell into an immediate and deep sleep. About 11:30, the telephone rang. It was my sister. All she said was, "Tom's dead". Tom had had an automobile accident on the way home.

The exact time that Tom died was the exact time I felt the presence. It wasn't my grandmother trying to get my attention. It was my bother-in-law Tom. I don't know what he was trying to say. All I know is that he came to see me. I suppose to say goodbye. Can I prove it? No. Do I know it? Yes.

Let me tell you about my mother. If you have ever been with someone when they die, you see that they just stop breathing. You go like, "Is this all there is?" "Is this what happens?" HELLO! I was waiting for something to happen other than just the last exhale. All I know is that one second she took a breath. The next second she didn't. It doesn't make any sense.

For the final couple of days before my mother died, I felt that something was different. Something was happening. Her breathing was a little labored. I didn't want to set the ambulance thing into motion. I hated the thought of all the sounds, all the blaring and the frantic action. I knew exactly what would happen. We had been down that road many times before. I just figured I'd get her hydrated and get her moving again. I do remember thinking that she must be dying. I remember thinking that something was different this time. I remember thinking that I didn't want to force her to go through a lot of drama. She appeared to me to be very comfortable and I also knew that she was not comfortable when strange people were in her presence. It made her nervous. I just didn't want all the commotion of sirens and strangers to disturb what I saw as serenity.

So I just talked to her. I constantly talked to her. She was afraid of sounds and I was very conscious of that. When I would walk down the stairs, I would say, "It's just me, Julia" or I would start singing so that she would know it was me. I didn't like to see her tense in any way. I surely didn't want her to be tense at this moment. I held her hand and tried to give her some ice cream. She just took a couple of deep breaths…and that was it.

I just held her. I was thinking that she was all mine at that moment and I was not going to rush the moment because this was going to be the last time. I waited for a couple of minutes before I called my sister. When I got her, I just said, "Mom just took her last breath."

I had asked for three things. Please don't let her die right away. I wanted time with her. Please let me be there when she died. I did not want her to be alone. I didn't want her to be in any pain. I got all three wishes. We were beginning our 5th year when she'd had enough.

When I think back, I remember that sometimes there were little peaks in her mental capacity. As I recognized those times, I would take off from work and take advantage of the opportunity to be with her. She could get much more lucid and verbal at times. I think on those moments as precious. I feel good about it but I find myself questioning myself. What more could I have done? What more should I have done?

One of the last things that she said was when she asked me to give her some eggnog. She said, "I like it!" I guess so. It had alcohol in it! That was back at Christmas time in 2000. We had fun. I asked her, "Julia, are you going to have a good day today?" Her answer was, "I don't know. Leave me alone." Another time, I said, "I love you, Julia." I purposely kissed her every time I saw her. She said, "I love you." Sometimes she would say, "Hello, darlin'." It boils down to those three things. She wasn't in any pain. She stayed with me for a long time. I was with her at the end.

So what does that make me think? Something happens on a spiritual level that separates our bodies from this existence. It blends with something else that is, in essence, almost never ending. Is it a reincarnation to a higher plane? I would really like to know what, if anything, happens to us when we die. Of course, we don't get that answer until the end. I find that I am really curious about *how* I am going to die. Exactly what is it that will end it all? The next question obviously is— What happens next?

I have felt at certain times in my life that if I had died at that instant, it would have been all right. The circumstances would have made it very natural because I felt what I might describe as a blending or a molding of some type of other force. Maybe I was thinking ethereal. My thoughts usually had to do with nature. It was something that was so beautiful and profound that I thought there couldn't possibly be anything else that could be as magnificent as the combining of my essence with something so natural.

As I described, when I was with my mother as she passed away, I was very conscious of what was happening. I was very aware of what I was feeling and what was happening. I asked myself; Will I get something from this? Will it be profound? Will there be some sort of a confirmation of what is happening right now? What IS happening? I realized there was something physical going on but I wasn't sure if I was attuned or aware enough to pick up on everything and gain everything I could out of the experience that I was supposed to. Will it be the same thing when I die? I think it has to do with where we are psychologically. How has death and dying impacted you generally and how will it impact us when we individually die? It is your solitary last trip. It's *your* trip.

I am curious about the crossings over of the people who are developed or who have the other sense of the connection of what else is happening. I have had my aura read. I have had astrological readings. I have talked with people who say they can tune in to other planes or other realms that could be defined as heaven. How we get there remains a mystery.

Is it significant to lead a good life? At the end, who directs where you're going? Where *are* you going? Is there a blueprint for getting there? I believe that religiously, everyone gets somewhere from a "God perspective" but you know, no one is assured of anything in particular but at the same time, I believe most, if not all theories have relevance. Are we going to meet up together somewhere or are different people going to different places? I sure hope it's a big time reunion but I guess I just don't see how that could happen.

Think about all of the different theories and beliefs people cling to. Think of the different things people think about. Are we all going to split up? We have been together all of this time on this earth but we have no assuredness that we will hook up with the other people we know and knew. I just hope we do.

I think I've probably seen a few things on Star Trek where they just went on to a different level of being. Perhaps it's simply another dimension…a mind meld if you will. Maybe there is a cosmic something that turns to light or energy …or a pureness that doesn't require a vessel…that connectedness that we feel in some people. We do feel a different connectedness with different people. Maybe that's it! Maybe we just have a great burst of energy …this big old cosmic mind. Maybe we just go to pure light. Maybe there is a black hole that everybody just gets sucked into that is pure light.

I don't know about walking around in robes. I don't know about the maintenance of a physical body. I really can't envision myself keeping my body but I do think I will recognize people from an energy. I do believe there is a recognition of some sort. I think we will go back into the big "soup" of things and that we will meet up on another level. I don't think it will be pearly gates or different types of landscapes. I think of it much more as a mental thing.

Thinking back on my mother, she used to have epileptic seizures. Afterwards, it was like an awakening...like shock therapy. It was like certain "things" in the brain were being reconnected. During the time I could still understand her, she was much more verbal and vocal. Sometimes, I would just sit there and hold her hand and talk to her. It was like Robin Williams in THE AWAKENING. I just have to think there is some kind of synaptic thing that is happening that mimics shock therapy for a brief time. There is something that reconnects.

I don't know if at certain times there is an energy. I believe that something does leave this vessel and that something is transported, diffused and absorbed into a larger kind of cosmic soup of all of us. It becomes a greater collected consciousness, a collected consciousness that maybe feeds into really what is one...something of a greater essence of what we are here for.

I look at the evolution of people or beings and you kind of have to ask yourself—— Is there a purpose? What is our purpose? What are we doing that makes this existence worthwhile? Is it being good and doing good deeds and moving on to a higher plane or *is* there a higher plane? Do we move ahead and evolve to something greater or do we go backwards and repeat because we didn't do such a good job?

I would like to think that you can evolve to enlightenment. I would like to think that there are levels of incarnation. I don't know the rules or regulations, nobody does. There are different theories and there are different parts of religions that deal with reincarnation. Of course, there are some religions that don't believe in it at all. I don't want to come back physically. I would like to go on to something bigger.

I believe that there is a higher plane of spirituality and that part of what you do on this level sets you on the path of something that is bigger than where we are and who we are now. I kind of look at how we treat ourselves and how other people evolve. I am disappointed in this existence or this plane. There really must be a higher evolution.

I find such beauty in natural things because they don't take on the characteristics of such ugly human type frailties that we have. Life should be beautiful but it's not. We can't get it right and I'm not going to live long enough to get it right. You think of your own sanctuary. I try to give myself comfort in my own physical and social surroundings. I have a great extraverted side but I also have a great introverted side.

It's really amazing when you think about it. You just have to wonder why people can't think of better things to do than hate. I just don't understand human nature sometimes. I find some escape and some wonder in science fiction. We could do so much better. We are so wasteful.

Back to death, I already have my plot. I have planned for it. I know what I want sung at the funeral. I find comfort in going to the cemetery but then I always have ever since I was a little girl.

Life is really blinks. I'm 55 years old. How many things do you really remember? There are moments, bits and pieces. 75 years old is not that far off in the whole scheme of things. Life speeds up. Living with someone who is old and dying gives you another perspective. How will you use your life? How will you take care of yourself? How will you dispose of your life? Who will it be disposed of? How will you be remembered?

You have lived 24 hours a day…365 days a year. There is generally a lot of time in a life but a life is not a lot of time in the evolutionary process. It's like two weeks. It comes down to…they couldn't even remember! There is a certain fear in how you will end your life. Can you remember it? Can you not even recall it? Where is that other place? Wherever it is, I certainly hope to reconnect to better times.

Will my body just be in Elmwood Cemetery (a cemetery in Detroit)? Maybe the body will be but the spirit won't. I think there is something on another level and I don't think it has to do with the images that we have. I think it's kind of imageless. I really don't have a vision of God. I have a feeling of existence but I don't have a visual. I have an essence. I have a notion. It is unperceivable because it is of another existence. It is not dimensional.

None of that frightens me at all. What it does is make me want to get my affairs in order. It makes me want to get my basement cleaned.

DYLAN

A couple of months after my brother passed away, I was so overcome with grief that I just cried. I was lying in bed crying but no tears were coming down my face. I'm not exactly sure if I was awake or not but all of a sudden I felt my brother Vandon smack me. He said, "Boy, stop crying!" That is *exactly* what he would have done. That is why I believe it really happened. I felt him smack me and I heard him say, "Boy, stop crying." It was exactly his method. So I believe when you're half asleep like that, your subconscious takes over and that's what tells you God is within you. I believe that spirits exist. I believe that is why I was able to hear and feel my brother.

If there is a hell, I believe it is earth. So based on what you do here on earth gives you your stature once you die and go on to another world. So those who do the right things or do well here, get higher up on the ladder. Those who do wrong things wind up on the bottom of the ladder.

I believe there is definitely a hierarchy in heaven like there is a hierarchy here on earth. As an example, I live well. I live in a nice house. I am comfortable. I like my house and my surroundings. I thank God for it everyday. Recently, my cousins came to visit me. They don't have a lot. They were very impressed with my house. In fact, they said, "What's it like to live like this?" It's a different perspective. While I'm comfortable, I don't think I have everything. But from my cousins' perspective we DO have everything. I believe a similar scenario happens in the next life. Your perspective from where you are is the same thing once you go to the next life. It all depends on what you do here.

I also believe that people who are evil or "wrong-doers" are necessary for society because it helps you know where the line is drawn. But here's the twist. Since we need the negative side, it's not fair to say the "wrong-doers" are going to a really terrible place, like hell. I think that terrible place was put in our minds to make us believe we have to do the right thing. It's a motivation or a challenge to do right. That's why I go to church. I don't feel if I don't go to church I'm going to hell. I go because I love God and I believe it is the right thing to do. It matters what we do here because what we do here dictates where we go after. If you are a decent and fair person, then you will have better positioning once you get to the next level. That's why you do the right thing. If you fail your life test, you go to the end of the ladder. You're closer to the devil than to God if you fail.

I know God and I'm hoping when I die I will still know God. I think that's important. I believe my brother smacked me when I was crying for him. He understood me and what I was feeling. He actually knew how to get to me. I do believe once you die, you still have the same memories in terms of what happens here in life. Those memories are actually clearer. I think you'll know everything and easily grasp everything once you leave this life.

My brother had become a deacon in the church. His eulogy was awesome. The story was told about an incident that happened years earlier when some kid dared to pick a fight with him. Vandon won that fight but after the confrontation, Vandon picked the guy up and took him to the nurse. After the boy was treated, Vandon was not satisfied with the medical attention. He thought the nurse could have done better. So he then borrowed a car and drove the guy home and then went back to school. I find that amazing that someone would do that much for his enemy.

Vandon has 2 sons. He always wanted a girl. They were finally blessed. His wife got pregnant and wouldn't you know they had a baby girl. Vandon died 3 days after she was born. Somehow that makes me feel that as sad as it is, Vandon did the right things in life. He passed his test. He finished the hell part of his life. Then, God said, "It's time for you to go". But He also gave him time to see his daughter. Vandon had a heart attack in her room. He died right there. I'm sure he didn't want to but he still had his bond.

We all have a sinful nature. I feel like I do better than most in fighting mine. God gave us a good side and a bad side. We have free will and choice. The battle is that we know what we are supposed to do. God lets us know that. But we have a nature that sometimes goes against His will. Here is the battle in life. If you conquer your bad side, you will have an upper level management job on God's team. I know I am going to have a good job in heaven. I just don't know what that job is. And that's what I will be doing tomorrow if I die tonight...whatever He assigns me. I will be high on His team carrying out His wishes. That's what I will be doing tomorrow.

MARGE

I know there is something beyond this. I have many explanations but I will share only a few with you.

MY FATHER

My father, whom I loved dearly and shared a very close bond with, died in 1953. He had suffered a series of strokes which affected his left side. It caused him to somewhat drag his left foot making a shuffling sound when he walked.

On the day of his funeral, I was presented with a crucifix and a rose from one of the bouquets that were on his casket. That evening, I placed the crucifix and the rose on top of the chest of drawers in my bedroom. Our home was on a corner with a streetlight. My bedroom faced the side street. There were only open fields to the rear of our home. The subdivision was fairly new at the time. The dirt road on the side street went beyond but the sidewalk pavement ended at the rear of our lot line.

I woke up during the night after hearing someone walking up the sidewalk from the front of the house toward my bedroom window. I immediately recognized the footsteps. I knew them so well. They were my fathers. I was only 21 at the time. I rationalized it could not be my father. The only way to quell my fear was to get up and look out the window. No one was there. I thought I must have been imagining the footsteps. I got back in the bed. The footsteps resumed. They finally stopped. I did not see my father. But I was certain he was there. The rose upon the crucifix lived beautifully for two weeks without water. In my youth and ignorance I later threw it away.

MY FATHER IN LAW

My father in law died at the age of 90. My husband was the executor of his estate. My father in law was a very particular person who managed everything precisely, meticulously and always in a very timely manner. My husband is also precise and meticulous but is inclined to be a procrastinator.

I became aware of a presence in our home shortly after his death. I could see the shadow of a person from the corner of my eye from time to time. Strange events were occurring. One example was the flatware in the drawer that would rattle loudly for no apparent reason. Subsequently, I asked my husband if he had settled his father's estate. He said he had not. I told him what had been happening and that I was convinced his father wanted him to complete the closing of his affairs.

He assured me he would tend to the matter right away. There were no more strange events for several weeks. They did begin again though, and again, for no apparent reason. Once more I asked my husband whether or not he had finished settling his fathers affairs. He had not. He told me there was more work to do. Once the procrastinator completed the last assignment, the presence left.

MY FRIEND

A dear friend whom I had known for many decades was ill and in a nursing home. She had spent much of her life studying about and acquiring antiques. She loved them. It was a hobby for her, a hobby she enjoyed for many years.

One mild December morning about 6:00 a.m., I stepped out on to the patio for a breath of fresh air. At that hour, it was dark and there was no breeze. Suddenly, before me, I saw this small antique oil painting. I'm not sure if I physically saw the painting or I saw it in my mind. It appeared to be about three feet in front of me. My friend loved that painting and I would have given my eyeteeth to have it. As I admired the painting, a wind chime began to ring softly although there was no breeze. I sensed at that very moment that my friend had died. I don't know what made me think it but that is exactly what I thought. I called the nursing home. My friend had just died. I went back out on to the patio. The oil painting was gone.

MY DAUGHTER

The loss of a child is a very difficult challenge. My daughter Judy died unexpectedly after a severe asthma attack. She leaves behind two daughters…lovely young women, Jessica and Danielle. Both of them were wrecked with grief but it seems that Jessica, the youngest, was having it particularly hard. The older daughter, Danielle, was pregnant. Her baby was due shortly after her mother's death. She also grieved for her mom.

Danielle was having a terrible time in her labor. Jessica and I were with her at the hospital. Something during Danielle's labor and delivery made Jessica especially sad. She was so sad she couldn't take it anymore. She left the room wanting to be alone but I wouldn't let her. I followed her. I thought it would be better for her if I was with her. I felt so bad for her. She was sitting with her head in her hands...distraught with grief.

It was a cold, early April evening. It was dark. It was about 9:00 in the evening. Jessica began to cry. It was one of those cries that came from the very soul...just a heartbreaking cry. She said between her sobs, "I wish Mom was here". At this point, I thought I saw something out of the corner of my eye. I turned and glimpsed a form. I could not believe what I saw. I saw Judy, my daughter. I stared at her to be sure I was seeing what I thought I was seeing. It was Judy. Her hands gestured towards Jessica. It was a very protective and parental sort of a gesture. She extended her right hand to her daughter in a very loving way. It was so touching and so moving. Jessica could not see this. She was facing the other way...still crying. At that precise moment, she said again, "I wish mom was here". All I could say was, "She is". It only lasted a moment. As quick as she came, she left. She stayed with me only long enough for me to see and interpret the visit.

There was also something else a little strange with this appearance. My daughter Judy was a very simple and casual kind of a person. She worked practically her entire life in the family frame business. She always wore blue jeans and sweatshirts or tee shirts. She hardly ever dressed up. She drove a truck. But she dressed up in her appearance. It was very unlike her. She had on a black skirt. Judy hardly ever wore skirts. She also had on a magenta cape. It came down to her waistline. I don't ever in life recall her wearing anything like that.

Her hair was absolutely perfect. It was beautiful like she had just come from the beauty shop. In life, Judy always wore it either loose or pulled back in a ponytail. She never fussed with her hair. But in this vision, her hair was absolutely perfect. That really stood out.

Judy had only died some 4 or 5 weeks earlier. With Danielle's labor so difficult and Jessica's grieving so intense, I believe Judy wanted to show them that she was still around them. I think Judy came to me rather than her daughters because she knew she could. We had always shared something of a mental connection. I could actually *think* at times, "Judy, call me" and believe it or not, she would call me...almost always at the moment I thought it. It worked both ways. Judy would send a mental request to me and I would pick up on it.

So when Judy appeared to me only weeks after her death, I was not at all alarmed. It was a very pleasant experience. My first thought was, "So. It's true. The spirit lives". I know this to be true. I know this was not a figment of my imagination. The very way she was dressed makes it all the more real for me. She was dressed unlike herself. For some reason, that was so significant for me. The concern on her face was so real, so sincere.

It was several months later that I talked to Jessica and Danielle about their mom's appearance. Jessica was awestruck. She seems to be more open to spirituality. Danielle was intrigued but she really didn't have a lot to say.

I have since dreamed of Judy. I use the word dream but that's not exactly what I mean. I was not asleep. I was awake and sitting when I felt her hand to my cheek. I have also felt her kiss my cheek. I felt so comforted by it. I can't tell you how comforted I felt. I knew immediately it was Judy. Can I swear to that? Do I have any proof? Certainly not. But I firmly believe it was Judy's presence and her letting me know she's OK and that I will be too.

Judy is still very much with me. She spent her life in this frame shop. She is still here. You can feel her presence all over this place. We should not be sad when someone dies. But we remain here in this mortal life and we know we will not see them anymore...at least not in this life. That's what makes it sad.

I believe we all enter a different dimension. I don't know what that is. There are all sorts of theories. I don't know that I necessarily believe in heaven and hell but I know there is something. If I died tonight, tomorrow I would be sitting in some beautiful place with lots of beautiful flowers and beautiful animals around. All of the people I have loved and lost would be there with me.

There is probably some trauma to dying. Your transition probably takes you a while. If I died tonight, I probably wouldn't know it as early as tomorrow. Time to us is set up by man...our clock and days and months. But the next "time" is probably a timeless dimension. An hour a day is important to us. It won't be in the next dimension.

NORMA

My mom was 93 years old when she died. She lived in a nursing home and had been there for about three years. We were all called in because she continued to get weaker and weaker. Her heart rate had dropped dangerously low. We stayed at her bedside talking to her, trying to comfort and reassure her. She kept telling me about her visions. She kept talking about seeing her father. Mind you, she was herself dying at the time. Right before her eyes closed for the last time, she had a big smile on her face. It was the brightest, biggest and most beautiful smile I had ever seen. She actually kept saying, "I can see Dad. I can see Dad." There was a glaze in her eyes. She was taking very shallow breaths. The smile was magnificent! Then, she closed her eyes and died. We figure her dad was the first person she saw as she left this world.

Although we could not see him, I know that she could. The experience made me feel wonderful. It made me feel peaceful. I am more convinced than ever that there is something more than this life on earth. We are not just here trying to make some sort of a life for ourselves. It's what comes next that's important.

I had another experience that has helped to form my opinions on life after death. I believe I died myself. I could feel myself floating very close to the ceiling and actually trying to utter a prayer. But the strange thing is, the prayer wouldn't come out. I saw myself floating on the ceiling looking at myself down on the bed. I woke up surprised and thought that I must have been dreaming. But it seemed so real. I could actually see myself. I could feel myself. I was right up under the ceiling. I remember thinking that my soul was going to pass right out of my body. But I was at home in bed. I woke up with a jolt. It was the strangest thing. I guess it was a dream. If it was, I thank God it was because now I have a chance to live some more. It was a dream, but it was not.

I consider myself a devout Catholic. I absolutely believe in the afterlife. I believe the afterlife is the presence of God. I believe it is the other side of hell. Hell is the absence of God. Heaven has to be total peace and the total presence of God. God created man to serve Him and to love Him. When we die, we go back to be with Him in heaven.

When I was a young child, I used to think that heaven was angels and harps and people were just there in each other's presence. But I think differently now. After a trip to the Holy Land, I got a real affirmation of my faith. Now, I feel that heaven is a peaceful place where you will see your loved ones again and your soul will be fulfilled because the presence of God will be there too. We should not be afraid to die. When I die, I want to have a merciful Jesus there to welcome me. I believe I will.

I know there is an afterlife. Part of life is a mystery. Part of the mystery is having faith. Faith tells me that Christ was born, suffered, died, rose again and is going to do the same thing for me. My body will rise up again when the time is right. This is not just a Catholic thing. All Christians believe this because it is true. We have faith that it is true.

Every night before I go to bed, I look at my calendar to see what I have going the next day. It allows me to plan my day. Then I get into bed and I pray that if I don't wake up, God will take my soul. If I am in heaven, there will be no time. If there is no time, I won't need my calendar but I will have all the time in the world to see my mom and my dad. I will see all of those who were my loved ones. It's part of the Christian burial right. I know that will happen. I sometimes wonder what we will talk about. We will be there for eternity and there will be no limitations so we will probably talk about everything imaginable. We can go right through a wall if we want to. And think about this. After we're glorified, when the Lord comes back again, well, there is going to be one big party. My thought is...where are all of these people going to go? That's a lot of people and one big party!

I cannot for the life of me, understand how anyone can believe this is it. Even if you don't specifically believe in Jesus, I can't see anyone believing only in this life as real. You have to believe that there is someone, something that makes this whole life program thing work. Faith is a gift. I'm so happy it was given to me. I pray for people who have no one to pray for them. No one is assured of anything and no one has ever really come back but I know there is life beyond life.

When I was in Israel, I got on a boat in the Sea of Galilee and I began to feel something special by being in the places where Jesus was. I felt just that being in the areas where He walked, where He performed His miracles, where He actually died on the cross... was the highlight of my life. It was an unbelievable experience. You cannot see and experience that and not believe. I felt His presence. I felt that whatever happened to me in my life, I would be able to bear it and endure it and then move on to the next life.

If you didn't think there was something better coming after this life, life would be unbearable. There is too much suffering. There has to be something better than what is on this earth. I believe this with all of my heart. I don't believe it because it makes me feel better. I believe it because I have faith that it is true.

I was with my husband when he died. We were in a restaurant and he just had a heart attack and keeled over. I felt in my heart that he was going to die. My immediate thought and action was to kneel down and whisper the Act Of Contrition in his ear because I just knew he was going to die. And he did. Right there...on the floor in the restaurant. I'm sure he left and went someplace better! The someplace better is clear in my mind. He went to meet Jesus. He was such a good person. That is very comforting to me.

If I died tonight, the first thing is that I would no longer be in the capsule of time. I would be in eternity. I don't know what I would be doing but my faith tells me that it would be fine.

CORINNE

How you spend your physical life, dictates how you spend your spiritual life. I believe that people go to a spiritual realm. You leave your physical body and take on a spiritual body. It's a switch. My husband was a physician. I think he is probably doing something that is somehow associated with the medical profession, his life's work on earth. I think when you die, you pass into whatever level you attained on earth. There is a relationship. What you did here dictates what you do there. You can pick up in the spiritual life, the way you spent life on earth. I believe there is a progression.

Some souls reincarnate. They come back because there are things those souls want to do on the earth plane. But it's not the same for everyone. Others die and stay on the spiritual plane and work from there. It's not a choice, though. You have either earned it or you haven't.

But here is something else. If you die and reincarnate, you will probably pick up some things on the spiritual side and use them when you re-enter the physical side that will help you in your next life. We all have certain things that we come into this life to do. Suppose you come into this life and you have a lot of bad luck. A lot of bad things happen to you. It's sort of like a payback from what you didn't do when you were here before...what you *should* have done when you were here before.

My greatest wish is that when I die, I will be able to communicate with people who I left behind. I want to be able to tell them that this is for real...you're not just wiped out. You really do go on to another realm. I believe that there are people

51

who die but they come back and show their images in different ways. Their loved ones know and recognize them and know that they are trying to communicate with them. Mostly they come back through dreams. It might be the only way. It certainly is the most common way. But I believe there are other ways as well. Let me give you an example.

My daughter Betty died almost exactly a month ago. I have been unbelievably sad. I lived with her. One day, I was lying on the coach. I can't explain it. I was not asleep but I was in another "space". I just felt different than I usually do. I thought I was feeling something coming from my daughter. I got up and started to write a poem. I was trying to capture the thought that began to gather in my head. Once I started writing, I realized the message was coming from my deceased sister. I kept getting these words in my head. I did not consciously think them. They just came into my mind and on to the paper.

VOICES OF SILENCE

This voice soft and gentle
Speaks to me of times gone by
Joyous days and memories of childhood
Wondrous days of growing up
And happy times we shared together.
Later, years of quiet times together
Talking of children, of marriage and of secret things.
Come to me again, O Silent One
And help me bear this loneliness
I bear alone now

At the time, I was not thinking! I wrote what just came into my head. It just came to me. I have no other way to explain it. It happened about a month after my daughter died. I believe my sister knew how sad I was and she came to comfort me. Here's the thing. I am not a writer. I couldn't write a poem if you paid me. I was lying on the couch. I was sleepy. Something made me get up and record the thoughts that simply started filling my head. That happened to me before. The other time was when my son died. A poem just started filling my head so I wrote it down.

Many years ago, I remember once being really sick. It was a long time ago. I had terrible pains in my stomach. My illness brought on a really unique experience. I know it was an experience of the Christ. Here's what happened. My sister and I went to Pittsburgh to visit a rather well known healer who had a church there. People would come from all over the country to visit her. I can't remember her name. Anyway, when we got there, there was a very long line. There was a line all around the block. She was on the stage of the church when we managed to get in.

This lady would talk from the stage. She would describe someone in the balcony and begin to talk about his or her illness. That person would then get up and go down on the stage. She would lay her hands on them. I didn't understand that then and I don't understand it now. But she would lay her hands on them. The person would fall and be healed. Now you might think that's hokey. Maybe it is. There have certainly been a lot of television programs that exploit the weaker minds and make money for the flamboyant. But at the time, it seemed right with me.

When I got back home to Detroit, I told my girlfriend (Pauline) about it. She was a Christian just like me. I told her I was impressed with what happened in Pittsburgh but I was not called upon and I still had these terrible pains in my stomach. We decided we should just ask Jesus if He could help me. I had that thought on my mind when I went to sleep.

I know I didn't wake up but I felt like I was awake. A real bright light had come into the window. I looked at it. There was this being standing there and I knew it was the Christ. I was always told and I always believed that if you prayed and were prayed for, you could be healed. I was praying for myself and my girlfriend was praying for me too. Anyway, the light was so amazingly bright. It's been 40 years now. I don't remember exactly. I just remember the light was extremely bright and the being was standing in the midst of it. Then it seemed like I woke up. When I did, the pain was gone. It was completely gone and I have never had it since. I would go back to that window time and time again and try to regain that experience…trying to have that same feeling. I never did. I never got the pain back either.

I want to impress on you how remarkable that experience was. My pain was almost unbearable. I couldn't seem to do anything about it no matter what I did and no matter whom I saw. But after my visit, it was gone! It was as if it was never there. Something, someone that night, took it away!

I have never been afraid to die. I'm not afraid now. My experience makes me feel "ok" about leaving this earth. My experience keeps me so interested and so intrigued with the thought.

Some time later, Pauline, our husbands and I were in Israel. We walked down into the Jordan River. We took our shoes off and held hands and walked into that water...the same water that Jesus Christ had walked in. I don't know if it changed anything for me but it was such a beautiful experience. It just made me feel good.

You have to remember this. How you act on earth, how you relate to people, what you do here, how you live your life determines what sphere you go to when you pass over. There are different levels but *you* determine the level on which you spend eternity. It's simple. Take a person like Hitler. He will be on the furthest realm down. Everything he ever did will come down on him. Take a person like Gandhi. He will be on a higher realm. You go to the realm you earn and deserve. If you know that and believe that, it will govern how you live. But if you think you're just here and you die and that's just it...then you're not going to be motivated to be such a good person. You have to believe. That, of course, is injecting an entirely different thought but all of this is tied together.

There are a lot of scholars who study metaphysical science. I don't think they are wasting their time. But most of the population of the world thinks that this is all there is. That's sad. I don't agree with that. I know that's not right. I can't prove it but I know it's not right.

I dream about friends that have passed on. One of them is Ruth Farmer. I have such good dreams about her. I loved her so much and I miss her so much. If I have had a bad day and I'm depressed about something, I dream about Ruth. In my dream, Ruth and I are doing the things that we used to love to do. We both loved to go shopping. We both loved to sew. That's what we do in my dreams. She said to me one night, "Come on, girl. Let's go to T. J's." She lifted my spirits when she was here and she is still lifting my spirits. My dreams about her are always good dreams. I don't think she's trying to tell me anything. It's just that she's still with me.

You know, when Ruth died, the same thing happened to me when my husband Biff died. It was strange. Seems like everything just drained out of me. I couldn't stand up. I couldn't walk. My daughter had to come over and sleep on the floor with me downstairs because I couldn't even get up the stairs. Life just washed out of me.

I believe that the relationship you had with a person on earth, determines the kind of dreams you have about them after death. If it was a good relationship, dreams are pleasant. If there were problems, unresolved issues, quilt...dreams can be unsettling and unpleasant. Sometimes that's difficult to deal with.

This is really something. When my mother passed, I remember thinking, I've got to figure this thing out. What happens when you die? I've been wondering ever since. She died 50 yeas ago. It's funny though. At that time, I thought, "That's all there is." I don't believe that now.

I am comforted by my thoughts now...thoughts that when you die, you don't die really. You continue on just in another form. I have faith. I know there is some sort of life after life on this earth. I don't talk with many people at all about this topic. Everyone is not open to this type of thinking. But my problem is, those who I would talk to are gone now. You have to have an open mind and understand each other. You don't want people to think you're crazy.

When I pass, I am going to try to let people on earth know I'm not just wiped out. I will try to let them know that life after death is for real. Our soul lives on…and it lives with other souls. Some people have the opportunity to come back. They do so through reincarnation because they have not finished their purpose. They come back to help other people.

I guess for some people, you have to have proof. People don't believe if they don't have an experience that makes them believe. Some people just have a feeling for it though. When one doesn't believe, he thinks those who do are crazy. I don't care what other people think about me. I know what I know and I know what I believe. I know what I have experienced.

We all have many, many lives. This one that we are experiencing now is just a stopping off point.

DUFFY

There is someone up there controlling our lives. I do believe we have free will. We have choices but I also believe there is a plan. There is a reason for everything. Nothing happens by circumstance. I believe God directed our lives…mine and my husband John's. John was Jewish. He was supposed to marry a nice Jewish girl. But that didn't happen. That is maybe not a big deal to others but in my life and John's life it was a "re-arrangement" that went against the plan.

Hospice sheds a lot of light on the dying process. Not only the physical dying process but also the psychological and spiritual side of the dying process. Hospice told us that people who are dying, very often before they die, they start talking about those who have gone before us.

John knew he was dying. A couple of nights before he died, he started talking about going fishing with his uncle, an uncle who had been gone for some 18 years. John had been very close to his uncle Ewie. John was an avid fisherman. So was Ewie. But John hadn't talked about him in years and all of a sudden he sees himself on a fishing trip with him. It was almost like Ewie was there calling to him.

My grandmother used to tell me that she would wake up with a start. She was 93 years old. She said she would see her husband, my grandfather, who had died in 1953. He was standing by her bedside. He'd say, "Edna. Come with me." And she'd say, "No, Frank. It's not time. I'm not ready to go with you. Go away." She told me this all the time. I believe it. I believe he was there. I admit maybe I want to believe it. Whatever! I believe he was there.

Lots of things happened when John was dying. The most significant was when my brother came in from Chicago. John would spend his day sitting in a big easy chair in front of the television. One day he said to me, "Duff, do you see the angels sitting on the couch?" I said that I did not see them. He continued, "There are two of them." He was as clear as a bell. He repeated the question insisting that "right here, right now" there are two angels sitting right in our living room on the couch in plain view. I tried very hard to see them. I tried very hard to imagine them. But I didn't.

John insisted the angels were there. He did not describe them. Understand that John was not a man who talked about angels and the like. It would be true to say that John had never started a conversation about angels. Who knows? Maybe he was hallucinating. I don't know. I can't prove anything. But he was adamant about it. I do know though that his comments gave and give me great comfort. He just kept looking. A short time later, he dozed off. Although I didn't see them, I'm sure they were there. John died a couple of weeks after their visit.

Also during that time when my brother was in town, we were standing in the living room facing the chair. I said to John, "Look who came to see you!" John welcomed him and said, "Marty, there's a bird on your shoulder." We were both surprised because we didn't see anything but John insisted. He said it was a little chick-a-dee. He insisted the bird was on Marty's shoulder. We saw nothing. John dozed off shortly after that…just like he did when he saw the angels.

I have another brother who is a physician. My brother was holding John's wrist and checking his pulse. John's heartbeat was dropping. It hit 50. Well, there was no doubt as to what was happening. John was dying. The pulse kept dropping.

Then, all of a sudden, it went back up. It rose to 100. We had a fabulous hospice nurse. Her name was Mandy. Mandy was so good to him and John just loved her. She did so many things for him. She was kind and patient. She was sincere and loving. All of this heart beat and pulse drama had been happening all night long. It was getting close to 8 in the morning. When Mandy came in, she walked right over to John and said, "John, I'm here with you now." John looked at her, smiled, closed his eyes and died within minutes. We believe he was waiting for Mandy to come.

The morning that John died, I was sitting beside him on the bed. He said to me, "Duff, I can't take the pain anymore. I gotta go." I said, "It's OK, John." He closed his eyes. We never spoke again.

At that moment, I left Mandy and the boys (sons) in the room with John. I went into the kitchen and looked out the window. It was April. There was a beautiful Michigan spring snow. John loved Michigan. He loved nature. He loved everything associated with it. He would never look out the window and complain about cold and snow. He would see it and feel it as beautiful. And it was. It was the kind of snow that comes down slowly and just sits on the tree limbs. It was very still. The sky was very overcast but you knew the sun was there trying to get through. But the snowflakes kept coming. It was 5 minutes after 8 in the morning. I remember feeling absolutely lost. I had no idea what to do. Right at that moment, my brother Marty came in and stood next to me. All of a sudden, he looked out the window and said, "Look!" There was this tiny little bird. He came down on the snow-covered branch and just looked at us through the bay window. It was just too weird because we had just experienced this thing about the bird on Marty's shoulder...

when John saw a chick-a-dee. Coincidence? Maybe. But I just found it so weird. The bird looked right at us and then it took off.

John was diagnosed with a very rare form of bone cancer. That was in September 1998. His doctor did not think he would make it until Christmas. It was so rare, I think there are maybe 10 or 12 cases in the whole world a year. But John lasted longer than they thought. He got a reprieve that went into April of 1999. The doctors said that it did not seem to have spread. John was thrilled. He got three months off before having to have another CAT scan. John had lost mobility in his right hand. He had nerve damage because of where the tumor was pressing. He couldn't write. He could do nothing with his right hand. But he spent the summer fishing. He loved fishing. He was so happy to be able to fish.

By October, John got really bad again. But he was concerned about unfinished business. He ran a building business. He had two partners. John was concerned about getting financial affairs in order and getting his name off the line of credit. He wanted to be indemnified because he was afraid that if something went wrong with the business after he died, they would come after me and the boys and his estate. John was obsessed with it. He would talk with his best friend and beg him to please help and get this issue settled. All related matters were finally resolved by a specific Sunday. John died the following Sunday. I really believe John would have died sooner but he absolutely could not leave because he was obsessed with resolving his unfinished business on earth.

At times, after John's death, I would be absolutely overcome with grief. Grief is a strange thing. It seems to come in waves. It's not a roller coaster. It's more like waves of water in the ocean. It comes with no warning. You can be happy as a clam and then all of a sudden the wave crashes over you and you are wiped out. One Sunday morning I was having a particularly bad time. I was driving to pick up something from the store. It was about 9 in the morning. I had the radio on. It was WCSX in Detroit. I remember the exact corner where I was. All of a sudden, I started to sob. I mean really sob. I thought to myself, John, just give me a sign that you are all right. I just need a sign. Well, all of a sudden, the disc jockey announced he was going to start a 3 record play. The first one was JELLY MAN KELLY. I knew the song well. It's by Livingston Taylor...the not so well known younger brother of James Taylor. John just loved James Taylor. In fact, we sang SWEET BABY JAMES at John's funeral. We had all of James Taylor's songs. We had Livingston Taylor's albums too.

Anyway, there is a line in JELLY MAN KELLY about "Jenny put the kettle on". John used to sing that line to the boys when they were little. There's a line that says something like "oh won't you come home" and something about "toast and jelly". The kids used to love to hear him sing it. Well, all of a sudden, here it is...JELLY MAN KELLY on the radio. I immediately knew John sent me that song. I asked him for a sign in the midst of my sobbing and here's JELLY MAN KELLY. Why else would they play that song? Hardly anyone has even heard of that song. Most people haven't even heard of Livingston Taylor. Weird? Yes. But it was a sign that gave me comfort and made me feel like he was there. I believe with all of my heart that John sent it to me.

Here is another thing. John, in the hospital bed in our family room, turned to my sister-in-law Julie and he said, "I'm going in six days." Julie said, "Where are you going?" He repeated, "I'm going in six days. I'm going home." John died six days later.

As sad as it is, I have often said I think everyone should live through losing someone like this. It is an unbelievable experience. You can talk and resolve your differences and know that the person you love is going to a safe place. John made it very clear that he was going to a safe place. He said he was getting on a second ship. He said two ships come. The first one goes to hell. He said the second one takes you to heaven. John said he saw the first ship come and go. I don't know where this ship concept came from but John said that's the way it happens. Your life dictates the ship that takes you away. John was not worried about himself. He was only worried about us...about leaving us behind. All he talked about for months before he died was making us safe. He truly loved us all.

If I died tonight and I could craft the perfect day tomorrow, I would be fishing with John. I believe we float up. We leave our bodies and we see it all happen. I think your spirit sees and visualizes everything. I don't know if your life passes before you   but I believe the spirit lives on.

LISON

I have a fascinating story to tell you but I have to give you a little of my history first. I am Haitian. My mother Sarah died when I was 21 days old. My mother was buried with a doll lying across her chest. The doll represented me, the baby she would never know. Haitian people are superstitious. The thought was that if my mother was buried with a baby, even though it was a doll, she would therefore not come to get her baby. As much as it was a superstitious act, it was also a protection for me, an act helping to ensure I would live a normal life in terms of length.

My father died when I was 3 years old. My brother and I were raised by my mother's cousin Lucille. I would dream of my mother often. Of course I never knew her really. I never even knew what she looked like other than through pictures. It's a strange thing really. It seems as though every time something was amiss in my life, my mother would come to me and reassure me in a dream.

My husband was in politics. Life was so unstable in Haiti that he would sometimes have to go into hiding or exile. He would be away sometimes for long periods of time afraid that he might be assassinated. That was very hard on me. With six children to take care of by myself, life could get very difficult. I was a very good seamstress. Often I would take in work and make money to take care of my family.

I remember I was having a very hard time one day. My husband was in exile. I was stressed about taking care of six children. I did not have many sewing projects so money was very tight and I was afraid. I cried all day long. It was just a very bad day. That night, I remember specifically, I was dreaming and in my dream some lady came knocking at the door. I sent my sewing partner, Janny, to answer the door. I told her that I did not want to see anyone. I just wasn't in the mood. I felt very depressed. Janny answered the door and told the lady that I was not home. She would have to come back. Well, the lady persisted saying, "I know she is here. I also know Lison has been crying all day." She told Janny that she must see me. Tell her I am here and that I am her mother.

When Janny gave me the message, I wondered how I might know she was my mother. I never knew her. Remember I was 21 days old when she died. But the woman at the door hollered in that I should look at a picture on the mantle and I would see that she indeed was the same woman on the picture, which was a picture of my mother. The woman at the door was the woman in the picture. She had a little infant doll she carried across her chest.

My mother told me that she knew I had been crying all day long. She said she wanted to stay with me for a while so that she could comfort me. I told her that she could not because I did not have any room. My mother reminded me that one of my sons, Jean-Jean, had a bed bigger than hers and suggested she might stay with him.

At that very moment, Jean-Jean woke up screaming. I woke up and ran into his room to see what was wrong. He was crying hysterically and insisting that someone had come in the room and got in the bed with him. He was 10 years old at the time. He said he felt somebody next to him and it woke him up. We sat up and talked endlessly remembering details of the dream and the experience. We both shared the same visit. My mother suggested a resolution to her request to stay and she carried it out. What is also interesting as well is the fact that she knew there was one bed in the house that was bigger than the rest. She was familiar with where we lived.

I dreamed of my mother other times as well. Whenever I became overwhelmed with what was going on, she would come to me in a dream. Every time she visited me, whatever was bothering me was solved shortly after. Sometimes it was even the next day that a solution to my problem arrived. We often had money problems and my sewing projects were not always steady. But after my mother visited, sometimes the very next day, I would get several projects and my money problems would at least temporarily go away. She was forever coming to my rescue. She always had the baby doll across her chest.

I remember one time I was visiting Les Cayes in the south of Haiti. My mother was from Les Cayes and she was buried there. I would always visit her grave when I was in the area. But this one time in particular, I neglected to visit the cemetery. I had many things to do and I didn't have any time. That night, when I was back at home in bed, I dreamed of my mother again. She asked my why I came to town and did not visit her. I still feel very guilty about not visiting my mother and I have never gone back to Les Cayes without a visit to the cemetery.

This is another story that has just no logical explanation. My cousin dreamed about my mother. In that dream, my mother told my cousin to give me a call and let me know that she was uncomfortable because there was a leak in her house. My mother told my cousin that when it rains, she gets wet. She wanted the leak fixed. I was uncomfortable when I heard that story. I knew something had to be wrong. I then went to visit my mother at the cemetery. I had her mausoleum opened and discovered that there was a hole in the roof. I had it fixed right away.

I have always believed that my mother watches over me. I used to get scared. I don't now. I always welcome her. She has been with me all of my life. I also believe that God uses my mother as a vehicle because He knows I will be comfortable with her.

SHELLY

Whoever put me together was asleep at the job. I have a lot of physical problems. I actually should have died many times during my life. I had a hole in my heart until I was 30. I have multiple physical internal anomalies. I have had 2 high-risk pregnancies. I lost a baby. But I'm still here. So that means there must be a God.

One of the weirdest experiences I ever had was my daughter's death. She was premature…15 weeks early. The whole pregnancy was actually a nightmare. When she died, my husband and I both felt something at the exact moment of her death…something that left us speechless. I can't explain this but I saw something. I saw something spiritual. I felt it. It took form somehow. I don't know how else to explain it. I saw this gigantic hand come out of the ceiling and lift her up… literally lift her up. I did not see it with my eyes. I think I saw it with my soul. I was holding her as she died. My husband "saw" it too. We weren't sleeping. We weren't dreaming. We saw the hand! Once it took her, I looked at her body and it wasn't her anymore. It was not Rebecca. It was just a body. Other people were in the room. Someone actually asked, "Do you feel something?" They felt it but they did not see it. I believe God came down to earth and took Rebecca to Heaven.

I had a dream later on…a dream that some might say represented my grief stricken mind but I believe it was a message from God. I saw a young woman riding a beautiful horse. I love to ride horses. Anyway, she was riding through an incredibly gorgeous meadow. It was an incredible scene in which I felt an indescribable joy. It was very comforting for me for a while. Somehow, I took it to represent peace for my infant daughter.

My grandma was 93 years old when she died. She had congestive heart failure. She knew she was dying. We all knew it. It was just a matter of time. Shortly before her death, she started talking about this being. She used to call this being a "guide" but a couple of times she used the word gatekeeper. She would say, "She's coming to take me away". She never appeared to be sad about it, she simply continued to talk about her female gatekeeper. This gatekeeper was a baby...a baby who was coming to get her and show her the way. She was very specific. She spoke of a little one coming to guide her. This happened about 4 years after the death of my daughter. My grandmother never stopped talking about this "little one". I believe that was my daughter coming through to help her with the transition. I have never doubted that Rebecca came back as an angel, or gatekeeper, to help us.

Our bodies are just something we live in. They house us. I am a spiritual being. I have a soul. If I was just a body, I might as well be a tree. There is no difference.

I know I will see Rebecca again. I can answer a lot of questions and satisfy a lot of curiosities. I will get to hear what her voice sounds like. I'll know what her favorite color is and what her favorite story is. I'd learn what she likes to do. I only had her for 2 days so I have a lot to catch up on. We'll get to hang out. I am a Christian and I have faith I will see her again. We don't just die and that's it. We're not just bodies. Look into someone's eyes. There is something else there. I cannot see how anyone can be an atheist. None of this is random.

You hear stories sometimes about people being helped in mysterious ways. They turn to look to the person who helped them to thank them from being harmed in some way...but the person wasn't there. I think of a phrase in the bible about always be kind to strangers because some have entertained angels unaware. That makes me think angels can take on human form. They do that for specific purposes on earth. They do their jobs and then they move on again.

There are also angels who constantly sing God's praises. I like to sing. I could do that for a few thousand years and I would be pretty content. I would also love to fly. That would be kind of cool. I can see all sorts of things to immerse myself in if I died tonight. The possibilities are endless.

This is another reason I believe in life after death. I work with sick people. One experience I had was with a 20-year old cystic fibrosis patient. She was dying. Her family was there. Everyone knew she was dying. I was sitting with her and her mother. All of a sudden, Judy (the patient) said, "Look!" She practically sat upright in the bed. Sitting up in bed was beyond her physical capability. She was very weak and sick. But she straightened up and insisted we "look". None of us saw anything. But Judy insisted saying, "Don't you see her?" None of us saw anything. But Judy insisted "she" was in the corner. "There she is." We looked and looked. Judy's eyes got huge. The expression on her face was happy. And then she died. She leaned back and she died.

If I could craft the perfect day after death, I would try to express my gratitude to God for giving me such a wonderful life. I would thank Him for my husband and my children. I would thank Him for my parents. I have a wonderful life full of love and comfort. After that, I would just look around in amazement because I made it. Heaven and the life hereafter is a gift of grace.

After I expressed my gratitude, I would do something outside. If there were a place like Glacier National Park, I would be there. I love being outside. Just put me on

So...What's Next?

a rock in the sun and give me something good to eat and I will be happy. If there is pizza in heaven, I'm going to eat so much pizza. Then, I'm going to hang out with my deceased relatives. It doesn't matter if everyone else thinks you're crazy. You believe what's in your heart.

WILSON

I believe that there is some sort of a spiritual afterlife. I have always believed there is some sort of a continuation. I believe it, if for no other reason, than because I have heard it all of my life. I also believe it because it's a source of comfort. It helps the idea of death become a little more palatable. Let me tell you a little bit about my background and maybe that might help to explain why.

I am the product of three generations of the African Methodist Episcopal church. Until I went away to college, I probably spent every Sunday of my life in church. My grandfather, Reverend James A. Charleston, was a very prominent A.M.E. minister. He was probably the most significant person in my life and in my family. Morally, I consider him to have been as close to an ideal person as one could possibly imagine. When you grow up under that sort of influence, when you could see how people responded to him, when you could see the effect he had on others, it is difficult if not impossible to eschew some of the principles that he had.

My grandfather died in the pulpit of his church, St. Paul A.M.E in Detroit. It was June 4, 1961. I was there. I was just 12 years old. I remember it was at the close of service. The choir was getting up to march out. He had a heart attack and he died right there in the pulpit. I remember being sad. I remember being frightened but because of the way I had been raised, I remember thinking that he had just gone to heaven. I remember the tears but what I didn't realize then, was that the tears were for myself, as they always are when loved ones die.

I believe heaven is a place of peace and joy. Since it is, I believe that my grandparents and my mother, my father, my nephew and the rest of my family are enjoying themselves and each other. I think each one of them is doing whatever it is that he or she enjoys doing. I believe heaven is multidimensional. So for my grandfather, he's fishing, going to baseball games and he is surrounded by all the books in the world that he did not have time to read. My grandfather loved to read so I have to assume that for him, heaven is fishing poles, baseball games, my grandmother and books. But if by chance he is looking down on me, I just hope that I have not done anything to disappoint him or any other of my family members in any way.

I believe that my mother's heaven would be having had her marriage succeed. She would be with my father and my grandparents would be in close proximity. Her divorce was the great tragedy of her life. She always loved my father. She never accepted her failed marriage. It made her view herself as a failure even though she was a highly educated and very accomplished woman. Heaven lets you change the life scenarios that affected you badly.

I have never had dreams or visions or felt presences but I will say that I think about my mother probably every day. I feel like I can actually hear her responding to things. My mother and I had a very special relationship. We told each other jokes all the time. Even today when I hear really funny jokes, I am saddened by them because I cannot go and tell them to her. My mother had a very difficult last six months of life. This is so funny. I was visiting her at the hospital and I told her a joke. She laughed so hard that it shot her blood pressure up. That threw off her respiratory readings and the alarm started going off. Three nurses and a resident ran into the room because they thought she was in trouble. She laughed just that hard. I was embarrassed to explain what had happened.

Here's another really funny story about my mother. My mother had a heart attack. For a while, she was critical. My sister Carole came to visit and stay with her for a while. Carole's son had died tragically in a car accident about a year earlier. Before my mother pulled out of the critical stage, we weren't quite sure if she would make it. But when my mother did begin to get better, Carole asked her if she had seen her grandson, Mikey. My mother said no, she had not. Later when Mother told me of the conversation, she described it this way. "Carole asked me if I had seen Mikey. Can you imagine her asking me that question? I told her NO! And I wasn't looking for him either!" We laughed and laughed and laughed but we also knew Carole was looking for signs from the other side.

My family is very small. So is my wife's. I loved my mother-in-law. I never had the pleasure of meeting my father-in-law. Everyone tells me that was my loss. I believe that our families should have the opportunity to be together forever. When my mother-in-law died, I had my father-in-law disinterred. I escorted his body as he was laid next to his wife. They are now buried next to one another. That's only about 30 feet away from where my wife and I will be buried. It is important to me that we all be together. I guess it's manifestation of some degree of existence in the hereafter.

You ask what I would like to be doing tomorrow if I died tonight. That's relatively easy. I would check with my parents. I would go see my grandfather and hope that if he had been watching me that I hadn't disappointed him too much. I'd see about my nephew. Then I would go and drink some whiskey with Herman, Allen and Jack.

So…What's Next?

Most people don't know this and maybe would not agree with it but I have always been a very religious person. There are things that I haven't done, not because I was not inclined, rather because of fear that I would somehow incur retribution. I think God will get in your face sometime. I spend a lot of time looking over my shoulder. I believe that if you do something that you feel to be morally or spiritually wrong, you could suffer the insufferable. I'm not exactly sure what that means. I don't know if it would be getting struck by lightening, having health problems or some form of sadness or lack of fulfillment. I believe that rewards are here on earth and sometimes so is punishment. I believe it so strongly that it moderates my thoughts and activities. I have an acute sense of right and wrong and I know how to control the two of them.

I am not afraid to die. But I don't embrace it either. As you get older, you realize you're closer to it than you are further from it. I think about it. I'm more afraid of getting sick than dying. I still enjoy my life. I still love and enjoy my wife after being married 33 years. We're not bored. I'm not afraid of what would happen after I die. My fear is the cessation of my life…because I am still having a good time!

CARL

It stays with me when someone I love passes away. I always keep the little memory cards. I have kept the memory card for every single person in my life whose funeral I have attended. It's just something I do. It's very important to me.

I'm an avid golfer. I was golfing one summer day. It was August 7th to be exact. I got a hole in one. That's a very big deal. Any golfer will tell you to get a hole in one is something very special. It usually happens once in a lifetime…if that much! After the game, I came home and for some unknown reason, I went to my box of memory cards. I don't know what made me do it but I just went into my home office and took out my memory card collection. My mother's fell out. It fell out! I did not take it out. I looked at the date on it. It was August 7th. My mother died on August 7th. I thought for a minute and realized the date still held another significance. Then I remembered my father-in-law died on August 7th. I immediately thought, "What a coincidence!" I don't know what made me do that. I have no idea why I went into the office and took out those cards…and especially on that date. Then I got to thinking, "Is that really a coincidence?"

I felt like it was some sort of a connection. I felt like they were all up there in heaven watching me play golf because they all knew how important the game is to me. I really had no conscious recollection that August 7th was an important date in my family. It just happened to be a date I played golf with friends. One of the biggest golf outings in my life now just happens to coincide with one of the most memorable dates in my family. It just seems strange.

I think maybe after death, there is some kind of spiritual "being" out there looking over you. There is somebody who sees things and is somehow involved in the incidents that occur in your life. I believe there is some type of a connection. I don't know what type of a connection it is. I don't know how it happens but it does happen.

I'll tell you something else. This has happened in my family. You have a thought. It enters your mind that someone has passed away. Then, out of nowhere, you get a phone call that not only has someone died, the person you were *thinking* about died. That has happened in my family a number of times. It's the strangest thing. Someone on one side of the country gets a conscious thought about the death of someone else who is miles away. You learn that as you thought the incident, it happened.

My mother remembered a very vivid such experience to me. I remember specifically many years ago she said that she thought for no reason that her sister in Buffalo died. Her sister was not sick so my mother said she had no idea why such a thought would come to her. She recalled a strange sensation coming over her and she remembered having the conscious thought that her sister passed away. Sure enough, a very short time later, she gets a phone call that her sister did indeed die. Why would that happen? I think there are forces in your life. There is no explanation as to why or how but strange, unexplainable things happen. It certainly makes you think that there is some sort of a continuance after life and into death. I don't know what forms it might take but there is something spiritual that is floating around that connects back to the person.

Here's something else that happened to me. I have had what I guess you might call an out of body experience. I left my body and was floating around. There was nothing peculiar happening at the time. I don't attach any meaning or connection to anything. It just happened...and more than once. I don't know why but I was able to actually fly around the room. It's almost kind of funny. There was no particular reason that I could think of. There was no place I had to go. I was just flying around the room checking out what was going on in the room underneath me.

I have thought about this life after death topic a lot. I am Roman Catholic. We are taught a lot of things about images and the Blessed Virgin. We hear stories of her appearing places and leaving messages. I have one myself. I was down in Clearwater, Florida visiting friends. My friend showed me something really amazing. He took me to a big glass office building. Burned into the side of that building was a very specific image of the Blessed Virgin. I saw it right there... burned into the side of the glass wall. There is no explanation of how or why it was there but it was. People have actually set up a little shrine at the base of the building. People from all over come and look at it. It's very clear. I don't know how to make it more clear for you. I saw it myself. It's about three quarters of a person. It's very clear. I don't know if it's even still there or not. But I do know that when I looked, I saw it.

That makes me think. I believe something is going on. Ever since she appeared, she has remained with me. I plan to go back later this year and I will look to see if she is still there. I believe that is a sign or a message, as there are other signs and messages that we see and hear walking the face of the earth. I believe spirits or forces or whatever you want to call them, are telling us to get our act together. We are not doing the right thing here on earth. There is some sort of a force telling us that we need to pray and ask for forgiveness. We need to repent, individually, each one of us. In my mind, that's what the image of the Blessed Virgin is telling us. We need to change our ways. I believe that until we make significant changes in the name of humanity, we will not be able to move forward.

I believe if we are good people here on earth we can go to heaven. I believe that one day, this world will come to an end. When? Who knows? But one day it will. The scriptures say we are going to have a thousand years of peace. We have to go through a lot to get there but life as we know it will end and the thousand years of peace will follow. After that, there will be no more life on earth. That's the bottom line. We have to get off of this planet. This world that we live in and all the buildings that are in it are like ornaments on a Christmas tree. It should be beautiful but it's not. The world is ugly. Everybody is always fighting and messing up everybody else's tree. In today's jargon, we just don't get it. That's why we have to get off of this planet. That's when things will be better.

There are some things that I believe or at least, am aware of because of my religion. We are taught about the miracle of the Fatima. The Blessed Mother appeared to three girls. One of them is still living. They heard predictions about devastating wars with each being worse than the last. Since that time, there has been World War I and World War II. There has been Vietnam and Iraq. It's scary to think about what might follow. The girls heard another prediction. The last prediction, or secret, was reportedly revealed to the Pope several years ago. We don't know what it's all about. The Pope never revealed it. That makes me believe something horrible is going to happen. Look at the things happening in the world right now. The Pope is reaching out. He travels to many different countries all the time trying to help people live their lives in the right way. He's trying to help us save ourselves.

80

We need to listen. All of us need to listen. Right is right and good is good no matter what religion you practice.

If I die tonight, my physical body will go to dust but there is also something else. There is a spirit or a soul or whatever you want to call it…that lives on. I think that is what the hereafter is. We go to another state. It seems to me that when we talk of Christ and religious people, they are in a different form and had to be transformed to a human form, something we could understand and relate to when they were on earth or when they specifically dealt with us. There are different levels of being that are totally different states. I don't believe there is any sickness or sorrow in heaven. We will have an existence with no problems once we take on that "other" level. That "other" level is not human.

I think that when I go to heaven, and if we are all in the same place, we will have some sort of communication. Otherwise, what's the purpose of being here? Are we just here to have a good time and that's it? And here's another thought. Heaven and hell are right here on earth. We make our own heaven and hell now. How you live your life and what you do in your life can be similar to heaven or hell. Everybody has their ups and downs and we all have our human frailties. We all have to suffer and go through tragedies because we are mortal beings. But there is something more than mortal. There is something higher. The higher level is where we will go.

Think about this. This is what I really want. I hope that when I die, the Lord and I would play a round of golf together. Wouldn't that be something! I'd lay back a little. I'd let the Lord win. Here's something else I have thought about that's kind of crazy. We, as human beings, dress different ways. We wear different things.

What do they wear in heaven? What kind of clothes do they have? Who makes them? Do they have tailors up there? Are they walking around nude or something? It may sound silly but they have to wear something!

I also believe there are different levels of heaven just as there are different levels of living here on earth. We are not all the same. I believe, and certainly I hope, there is something next. As we try to live our lives here and try to find our purpose, and strive for success and happiness, we constantly learn things. We try to attain various levels of life. I think we will do the same thing in the hereafter. It's like different kinds of love. If you are fortunate enough to have a good marriage, you live your life with love and you treat your kids with love. Then you have grandchildren. You love your grandchildren but in a different way or on a different level than you love your own kids. It's kind of a pure thing. We create families that also create families. Generations of families are very special. Families are extensions of who you are. Future generations are a happier state. Your existence in heaven will be like that extension. It's like a future generation. It's a happier state.

The afterlife is going to be great. Just imagine, we will be free of prejudice. We will be free of hate. We will be free of pain. There is no room in heaven for all of that negativity. We, as human beings here on earth, just don't get it. But when we hit the next phase, we will get it…true meaning. And play golf or not, we'll all be happy.

WALDO

I think like Dr. Kevorkian. After you die, you rot. Unless you are mummified, you rot. I don't believe there is any other side. One of the most difficult things anybody could be asked anytime is "Is there a purpose to being here?" I don't know. I don't think we can truly answer that question. I believe that there is a supreme being someplace. But as a supreme power as portrayed commonly, as a father figure with a gender, I don't believe that.

People wonder if there is no after, then why is there a before? I don't know the answer to that either. The question is simply too complicated to answer. I don't have a deep, philosophical mind to deal with that question which is why I think most of us avoid the question "Why are we here?" I don't know. I have no answer. I sit around with a bunch of guys just shooting the breeze and talk about exactly that. I don't think anyone has an answer…at least not one that I've found satisfactory. I don't think we can say "Why are we here" anymore than we can say, "Why are ants here?"

I have never felt the presence of anyone who has passed away but I have talked to people who believe that they have experienced the presence of someone dead. My mother believed she had an extra perception. We had 12 children in my family. Most of my brothers had left home and gone to different parts of the world when I was still an adolescent in Alabama. Somehow or other, my mother knew when one of my brothers was in trouble. They could be in Michigan or Kentucky; it didn't matter. I had 3 older brothers who were gone from home at the same time. My mother knew when something was going wrong. My brother Hayward was a brick mason. He was working in Detroit. He was able to get a job for Tom, my second oldest brother. But Tom was a street hustler. He could only hold a job for about a week. He was running with some absolute thugs. One day, the cops picked him up (this was way back in the late 30s). When the cops picked up Tom, my mother knew it. She didn't know the cops picked him up but she knew he was in trouble. She called my brother Hayward before he could even call her. That is my only experience with someone who had some extra sensory perception...or a wireless connection with something out there.

My older sister Betty thought she could do that too. She always felt she had extra sensory perception but I never saw her demonstrate it. Other than my mother's experience, I just don't believe it.

I loved my mother. I miss her. But I don't ever think I will see her again in any form. I don't believe in the hereafter. I don't believe in communication with the dead. I guess it's because of basic science although I know that there are people in basic science who believe. Others have a lot more spiritual make than I have. It doesn't make me feel sad. That's just the way it is.

I guess the unfortunate thing might be that I was raised in the Baptist church in Alabama. I came to Detroit when I was 13 years old. I had so many things drummed in me as a little child for as long as I can remember. We would go to Sunday school at 9:00 and then to church at 11:00. Then we'd go to BYPU (Baptist Young People's Union) at 5:00. I had this stuff drummed into me. My family was fundamentalist Baptist. They had prayer meeting on Wednesday. This was so dominate and forceful in my life from such a young age that when I got to start thinking for myself, about 12 or 13, I decided I didn't believe all that stuff they were telling me. I still don't.

Some people use the word "miracle". It depends on what you mean by the word miracle. I remember something that happened to me early in my career...maybe 30 or 40 years ago (Waldo is a medical doctor). It is why I never discuss religion with my patients. A lady was sent to me many, many years ago. She needed a very complicated operation. I believe in informed consent. So, after I reached my conclusions, I would sit down with my patients and talk to them. I spoke with this specific patient. She was very ill. The operation would be difficult. I explained to her exactly what we needed to do. I explained everything with as much detail as I could. When I finished, she said "If we come through this, it will be a miracle!" I then made a big mistake. I told her, "I don't believe in miracles". I never saw that lady again. She no longer wanted me to operate on her because I told her I did not believe in miracles...and she did.

A miracle to me is something that happens and you can't explain it. It's a word that is tossed about lightly now in the press and in general. I don't believe in miracles. My basic belief is that everything can be explained. We don't always understand it at the time but there is an explanation. Many things that we used to think of as miraculous happenings are common knowledge now. 60 years ago or whatever it was, if you talked about someone walking around on the moon, you would think that impossible. A miracle is when there is a situation on earth where nothing physical can explain it. There IS an explanation.

I think everything is circumstance. I don't think there is destiny or predetermination. I first met my wife in medical school - at Meharry Medical College in Nashville. It was in anatomy class. It was a hard class. I remember seeing her crying one day. She wanted to go home. The only reason she didn't go home was because she didn't have enough money for train fare. She knew if she called home, her father wouldn't send her the money even if he could. She also knew she couldn't get anybody in our class to loan her money. It's simply coincidence...circumstance. We were simply freshmen together in anatomy lab. She came of her free will. She couldn't leave. I happened to be in that class. We got together.

I have had patients who were on the brink of death for a long time and didn't die. I have had patients who were on the brink of death and did die. I have never had anything happen to me in my surgical lifetime that was miraculous. I have had things happen that I thought to my great good fortune or to the patients' great good fortune happen. I have been at home in bed and woke up suddenly and thought, "Oh my God!" - I should have done this or I should have done that. I would get up and run back to the hospital and do something that I think might have been a factor in a patient's recovery but I don't think that's a miracle. I don't know what happened to awaken me in the middle of the night to tell me to do something but I still don't think it's a miracle. Had that not happened, the patients might have had a different outcome and even died. I don't know what you call that...but not a miracle.

I was discussing a case with a lawyer who did a lot of malpractice. He asked my opinion about a specific doctor being sued. He wanted to know what the doctor did or did not do in terms of it being proper procedure. He asked what I would have done under the same circumstances. I replied that what the doctor in question did, did not breach the standard of practice even though it might not have been the same thing that I would have done. I say that to say that you do some things and you make some decisions that are the result of a whole lot of factors...and things that wake you up in the night are a combination of a whole lot of factors.

I feel peace within. I am at peace with myself and I am at peace with my professional past. I love what I did. I enjoyed is so much, I used to tell my wife, who is also a physician, I would operate for free. I had fun everyday. I loved my professional life.

I am not a spiritual person. My family thinks otherwise. They are very religious and spiritual. My wife is and my daughters are even more so. My parents were fundamentalist Baptists. Historically, I believe in recorded history. I believe there was a Jesus but I don't believe he walked on water. He taught. He preached. I don't believe quotes in the Bible though. Who was walking around with Him taking notes? But I believe philosophically there was a man called Jesus. I also believe the way the western world depicted Jesus is wrong. There was never anyone from Asia who was blonde and blue eyed.

I believe that there is a supreme power somewhere but so far as we know, it's formless. From the beginning of time, we talked about the heavens. Everything we talked about was up. There are many more galaxies out there. The earth is just a little speck. I think there needs to be a belief in the teachings of Jesus and Mohammad.

If I died tonight, I would be rotting in my grave...unless I was mummified. Dead is dead and gone and nothing. I wouldn't be doing anything. As far as I'm concerned, the undertaker would starve to death. We have all kinds of rituals of what to do when we die. We spend a whole lot of money for funerals. It's a waste. I do not believe in the hereafter. I recognize that is contrary to the majority of beliefs in the world...but it is my belief.

STU

It's taken most of my life to be absolutely certain but I know there is definitely a spirit world. I have had two experiences that confirm what I suspected all along.

I got sick and went down. I had two heart attacks in the same night. I had one heart attack at work and the other at the hospital. The one at the hospital happened as I was being taken to the cardiac care unit. I was actually chipper and in no pain until the second attack began. I had seen my family in the emergency room and was not particularly frightened. I was concerned but I was really thinking about the fact that I was going to have to quit smoking.

But the last thing that I remember until later in the week was being taken off the gurney and being placed on the operating table. After that, nothing. Nothingness. As I thought about that – no out of body experience…no white lights…it frightened me. Later I found out that I had three arrests on that table.

I learned two lessons from that. If your heart stops, you don't gradually fade. You don't have time to wave goodbye or to make your peace. It's lights out! That's it. That's the first thing. It doesn't hurt. It's simply nothingness. I woke up in the middle of a catheter procedure with a breathing assistance mask on my face. It was uncomfortable. I fought to get it off. I recall the lights going on and off. That's actually a part of the procedure. They turn the lights on and off so that they can see the pictures better. I remember that I wanted them to hurry. I said that clearly to the team working on me. I didn't know what they were doing but I wanted them to stop. There was a camera that was moving about me. It was making me a little claustrophobic. But the thing that I remember most clearly (and I didn't understand it then – it took five years) is that I experienced a physical/psychological sensation. It felt like a release or a calming sort of a sensation. It was very peculiar. In fact, I said to one of the attendants, "I feel very peculiar." I did not understand it.

Fast forward five years. We had just placed my father in a hospice. He had been in home hospice care but it was recommended to us that he go into a residential facility. His breathing had changed. He had a small stroke. I was visiting him a few days later. The family was all around him. My mother was there. His brothers and sisters were there. So were his grandchildren.

For some reason, I began to feel very, very bad that day. I was ill. And I thought for a while maybe it was something I had eaten. But my lunch was reasonable. I decided that whatever I was feeling was not related to food. I began to think I was not going to be able to finish my shift. I began to feel just awful. That was around 5:00. I began to struggle with what I had to do. About an hour later, my sister called me with the news that my father was dying.

As I left work, on my way out to my car in fact, I recall speaking to my father through the grief. I said, "I'm on my way, Dad. Wait. I'll be there." I got in my car and as I drove, I still felt awful. And as I drove out on to the highway, I looked at the clock and about 6:24pm, the same sensation that I had experienced 5 years ago came over me again. It was the peculiar feeling I felt in the hospital when I had my heart attack. I felt peculiar. Not ill at this moment …peculiar. I don't know what prompted me to say it out loud but I said to my father, "It's OK. If you need to go, go. I understand. Don't suffer. Go." Slowly, that peculiar sensation left me. I then began to feel alive and well and calm…sad, but calm. When I got to the hospice,

I was told that he passed away at 6:29, which, of course, was 5 minutes after my peculiar sensation began.

I am convinced. I don't know if it was my father's spirit or an angel or what but when I was in my car, I was in the presence of someone related to the other world. And I understood then that the experience that I had had on the operating table was that I had begun to touch the spirit world. I hadn't gone but I sort of had one foot in and one foot out. It took me five years to understand that I touched the spirit world. There were no lights. There was no out of body experience. There was however some sort of a connection. I believe that on the operating table, someone touched me. Maybe they were there to pull me from the brink.

I was terrified before I connected the two experiences though. Before my two experiences, I was afraid that what happens is just oblivion. After the experience on the operating table, I don't remember a thing. Just darkness. I only remember waking up briefly and having that peculiar, restorative experience. I don't remember anything else until I woke up in the middle of the week.

Last summer, my aunt passed away. We had a memorial service for her shortly after. Her youngest son Bruce spoke at the service. Afterward, he said to me, "I know she's gone. But she's here. I can touch her. She's just on the other side." He said, "There's a veil" as he gestured to the air. I think I understand that.

Shortly after that, during my daily walk, I was thinking about my father. I loved him very much. I share his name. I have always believed he was my first and best friend. He suffered with ALS but he stood up to his disease with joy and with a smile on his face. He was never cross. He never complained. Up until the day of his death, he got up and got dressed. He never gave into it. He actually never even talked about it. I couldn't understand the courage he had. I didn't know where he got it. His father died of the same disease. So did his half sister. He saw it in others. He knew it was not going to be easy. I don't know how he could stand it. Anyway, as I was walking, I heard him say, "The courage, I got it from you…from your mother, from your brothers, from you." He answered my thought. I heard it clearly. That makes me believe that some spirits stay for a while to help those who are troubled most by the loss. He helped me pull through. I hesitate to tell my mothers and brothers about that because I don't want them to think he favored me in some way.

All of this comforts me. My peculiar feeling…it's sort of restorative. A restoration of spirit and psyche…something. At any rate, I have felt the presence of my father. There were many times in my life as a child, I went to him. He always seemed to have the answers. He also had the answer when I struggled to accept his death.

Sometimes when visiting the gravesite, I walk around and look at other graves. I was struck by one headstone which read: DON'T WEEP FOR ME. I AM NOT HERE. I AM IN HEAVEN. It made me think. Do I have a concept of Heaven? The answer is no. It's too mysterious. I just hope they have music.

PAT

I feel like my great grandmother, my grandmother, my mother, my sister and my auntie are sitting on a cloud somewhere watching me. I feel them. I suppose my expectation is that I will see them one of these days. My mother always said she would be sitting on a cloud watching me so that's the visual I have. I think we will all be together swinging on a cloud. At least that's what I hope I'll be doing.

My sister Linda died in 1975. She was murdered. It was a horrible ordeal. It was devastating. My mother died some 18 years later. I remember thinking when my mother died, that it was OK because I really believed that she was finally where she wanted to be and that is with my sister. My mother could not stop grieving for my sister. The only way to put an end to that horrible grief would be to join her. My mother was so convinced that once she died she would be with Linda again, that I began to strongly believe what she said as true. To this very day, I still believe that is the case. She hurt so badly there was no other way she could feel peace.

My sister's murder case went unsolved for 15 years. When the case finally did come to the forefront, my mother said that she wanted to let Linda know that she could come out now because the bad guys were caught. She could come back. I guess for her, that was closure.

When my grandmother died, my mother's mother, MY mother missed her terribly. She was convinced that one day she would be with her again. I've been around that kind of thinking so long I guess I must have internalized it. It is sad when people die but it really shouldn't be because in a strange way, it really doesn't matter. It's just a matter of time until all people who loved each other will be together again.

I think that there has always been something inside human beings from the beginning of time. Civilizations have always buried their dead. People were not told to do it. We just did. When we go back in history and find ruins and burial places thousands and thousands of years ago, we realize burials have always been a part of life forever. There has never been a time when we didn't take care of our dead one way or another. Practically all civilizations have done that. We still do.

They say that no energy is ever lost. No matter is ever lost. It is only changed. So our bodies go through a transformation and physically die. But it's just a body. It is not the person. The body instantly becomes this inanimate thing. It collapses on itself. The energy is gone. It's dead. You KNOW it's dead. It's different. You look at it differently. You now see it as a shell. It's a dead body and we all know what happens. Ashes to ashes and dust to dust. The worms eat you. You become compost. It's part of the cycle of life. But remember, I am talking about a "body".

What about the spirit? What about the life force? Where does that go? Maybe it just evaporates and becomes part of the atmosphere. Who knows? I think it goes somewhere. I think it's held somewhere. Maybe that's how we recognize each other on another plane or another level. The spirit, the intellect, the spark of humanity lives on. It's like a sentience or an awareness. The life force does not go away. Maybe that's an explanation for things that happen that you just cannot explain. You become aware. I just can't believe the spirit goes "poof". I can't believe all we go through, all we think about, all we plan, all we discover, all we learn, all we know and care about just goes away. I don't know what form it takes. Maybe there is another dimension. Maybe there is another parallel universe. I just don't believe we disappear. Matter doesn't disappear. It changes.

Sometimes I dream of my mother. I use the word dream but it's really not that. I refer to it as a visit. Sometimes I can smell her. I can smell the perfume she used to wear. I can feel her. I might even say, "Hi Mom." She is so with me. I know it's something like a dream but I also know she's with me. It's just so real. They are such good "dreams".

I also used to dream of my sister. I don't anymore. I believe she chooses not to come to me in dreams. I believe that she knew I was scared. After she was murdered, I couldn't sleep. I was horribly frightened. I think she knew that. So she stopped coming. I thought once I saw her at the end of my bed. I felt her presence. That was her last visit. I think she forgives me for being afraid.

When someone dies so horribly, so violently, it tears a hole in the family. It's a hole so big you can walk through it. It doesn't ever go away. You just learn how to live with it. You incorporate it. Their children become your children. The spirit lives and it comes through in other ways. Many years later when her son had his first baby, it was a very big deal in our family. The first time I held that baby, my nephew's baby, I felt like I was channeling my sister and my mother and my grandmother and great grandmother. I feel like I am holding him for all of them. I feel like they are around me. I talk to them.

There is never any closure really. You never get over the death of someone you really love most especially if it's a tragic death. There is just the constant pain you learn to live with. In time the edges soften but that's about the best you're going to get. There is not a day that goes by that you don't think about it. There's not a day you don't compare things to it. It becomes a benchmark. I hate going on an airplane. But I think if this goes down, it'll be a better way to die than my sister died. Her death was a real turning point in my life. Her death made me look at life an entirely different way.

They say that if God didn't exist, it would be necessary to invent him. I don't believe in God as most people do. I believe in God as the circle of life, the earth as mother. That makes more sense to me than Jesus or any of the other male oriented religions. Life everlasting, resurrection, pearly gates. Nah! That's not what I see. That's not what I feel. I feel it's more than being in each others' presence. I believe that souls or spirits or vapor will recognize each other in the phase after death.

Anyway, if I die tonight, tomorrow I think I'd be hanging out with Linda, Mom, Mimi, Auntie Dee and Dodo. I'd like to be watching everybody down here. I'm hoping that I can be a helpful presence. Like I said, I have a visual of swinging on a cloud, the visual from my mother. She told me she would be watching me. I'll be sitting on a cloud. We'll be together. That would be my favorite thing. I'd be with my family.

DEBORAH

If I died today, I think that tomorrow I would be looking down on the people who were part of my life and I would see how they are reacting to my death. I'm sure the circumstances of my death would play a part in that. Actually, if I died today, it would be unexpected so I would imagine that people would be upset. But in the long run and for what ever reason, I would think that because I am relatively young, I would be sad and so would those who love me. I would miss out on being able to share experiences and events with the people I love. There is so much left to live. While I am anxious to see people I loved who have passed on, I still want to be a part of what's happening here, now.

So except for the regret for leaving the people you love, I would like to think that when you die, you are basically at peace. Because you are at peace, you can go and look for those you have lost. I believe there is a heaven. I believe heaven is whatever makes you happy. It is what you want it to be. I want it to be a place where I can see all my deceased relatives and friends.

Heaven is a state of mind. I don't think it's walking on clouds and angels all over the place. It is what I want it to be. Therefore, it is a place where I will be back with my family. We will all probably be in a house or a park or someplace that was significant to all of us. Can you just imagine being what you want to be when you want to be it? I could be 6 years old living on Edison Street in Detroit. That's where I lived when I was a child. My family was together. I remember everyone being very happy. To re-live that time and to have my parents with me as I remember those years would be absolutely beautiful. It becomes a spiritual thing…something like the spirit leaving the body…something like a state of mind.

So...What's Next?

The very first people I would look up are my mother and father. They would take me to the rest of the people that I want to see. After that, I would be able to see whoever came to my mind. I think of my dear friend Herman Kelsaw. We were great friends in college. He is my first friend to have died. He died when we were in school. I think his death was unnecessary. I have been mad at Herman for all of these years…for the past 25 years or so…because I think he did something stupid.

Herman got into a swimming pool and he should not have. I don't know if he had been drinking. I think he may have gotten disoriented. I have questions about his death. I believe he may have faced a challenge and for whatever reason, he just gave up. He had a tendency to say "forget it" if he was not doing as well as he knew he had the potential to do.

After Herman and I get caught up on all of the lost years, I would ask him to take me to Bobby Gunn. Bobby was another college friend who died too soon. After we finished talking, I would look up other people and catch up on old times.

I'm kind of mad at my father. It wasn't his fault that he died but I missed him terribly. I was so young at the time. I was 12 years old. I still miss him. My mother did too. I just want to be with him. I think he looks at me now and he wants to be with me too. I think he talks to me and he has tried to get in touch with me. This is kind of funny but I like to think he can only see me when I am doing something good. I have done a whole lot of stupid things in my life but I guess if someone loves you, it really doesn't matter. They love you regardless of what you do. But I like to think when good things happen, loved ones who are gone are a part of it too.

I believe my father may have given me some direction at different times of my life. My memory is sporadic. Again, I was only 12 when he died. He had been away in the army for 2 years. I was 4 to 6 years old at that time. I missed so much. I have an awful lot to catch up on.

If I could design the perfect day, I would be living on Edison Street in Detroit. My parents would be there and our family would be together. People that I didn't know, people who I heard my parents talk about would be there too. We would have just a huge family reunion. We would have a lot of good food. We would have a lot of people with a lot to eat and drink. Why? Because that is exactly what I want.

I think I have led a fairly decent life. As it relates to what happens next, I guess I think about what the perimeters might be for heaven or purgatory. I don't think there is a hell but I'm sure there are delineations. Just like there are different neighborhoods for different people, there are different levels of life after death. There could be someone I want to see or be with but I might not necessarily get to be with them because we might not be on the same level. I really wonder about that. I think there could be different levels in heaven and where you go depends on how you lived your life. Could I possibly be in the same place where Mother Teresa is? I haven't done anything as wonderful as her but at the same time, I haven't really done anything horrible either. So that reasoning says I wouldn't be wherever Hitler is. But if for some reason he does happen to be where I am, I just don't want to see him. If God has forgiven him and has a place for him, I just hope I won't be in the same place. Just think, wherever that place might be, some of the other people there might not be as forgiving. There *is* a whole lot to forgive.

I wonder about religion. I am not Catholic. Because I am not, I cannot go to confession and communion and, according to that faith, be forgiven. Is one not allowed forgiveness because he or she is of another religion? With that as a backdrop, I would like to think that there is something in place here on earth, that there is a definition for good and bad...and therefore some sort of a formula for where people will go.

Most people are basically good or bad but the question is *how* is that decided? Who makes that decision? Going back to Hitler, if he really thought he was doing the right thing, if he really did what he believed in as right, is that a consideration? I simply cannot accept that. Whatever the circumstance, if you are killing people, even if you think it's the right thing to do, you are still killing people. I just wouldn't want to be in the same place with someone like that. But then again, I went to college with some people I wouldn't want to be in the same place with either.

I sometimes have a conversation in my head with people who have died. I guess I started doing that with my father. I have to have a conversation because I am not a cemetery person. I don't think that's particularly necessary. Something about that makes me sad though. I don't know what. Sometimes I dream. Sometimes it seems so real. It's just so disappointing to wake up from a beautiful dream. It's too bad they can't last forever and ever.

I find myself thinking about all of the things my mother told me. I had her so much longer than my father...about 40 more years or so. I wish I had listened better. I wish I had done more than just say "Yeah" and sloughed it off. I'm not necessarily talking about words of wisdom. I wish I had even paid more attention to gossip, what people did and where they used to live. The longer you live, the older everyone gets and you find you have no one to ask about things.

I think about burial and funerals. My mother always said she didn't want to be remembered sadly in other peoples' memory. She didn't want people to see her for the final time and see that she was sick and tired. She would rather they remember her in better times. I agree with that. My husband and daughter know that I don't want my casket open. They can see me for closure if they have to but no one else can. I guess my mother put that thought in my head. It's still there.

After all is said and done, we don't like to think about dying. Still, we do think about it though. I just hope that when good things happen, my parents look down and they are happy for me. I hope my friends appreciate good things when they happen too.

LOU

Everyone has schooling in death and dying. If you have lost anyone, you have been schooled. It may not be a formal sort of an education but it certainly is a home schooling of sorts.

I don't have a particular feeling that there is a specific place we're going to go. Christians are raised to believe there is a heaven and a hell. Good guys go here and bad guys go there. But if you're a thinking person, you realize no one religion has all the answers. I think religion has been shaped to fit our personal needs and to reassure us in times of doubt. But more than anything, I think there is an energy source within everybody and that energy source is eternal. It's not going to go away.

I have been in a position where I have observed people dying. I have had some occasions where I have given that person permission to die. I have been the one who says, "Go ahead. Let go." In a couple cases, that person died right then. I believe they heard me.

The last time I was alone with my wife's mother, she said to me, "They are not doing this right." She appeared to be really angry. She kept repeating that the people around her were not acting in the right way. When I asked what she meant, she said, "You know what I mean! They're not helping me go." I tried to comfort her by agreeing with her thought and even suggesting that she just relax and let go. About 10 minutes later, that is exactly what she did. She let go. She died.

I was also with an uncle when he was about to die. He was in a lot of pain. I just told him to let go. He asked when. I said, "Immediately". His wife, my aunt, was also there. She didn't want to let him go. He felt she was holding him back. When she left the room, he died. I believe that those on their deathbed are looking for permission. When they feel they have found it, they let go. I believe we have that control.

I was with my first wife's stepmother when she died. We were good friends. I liked her. She had problems with others because she was not the first wife and that can sometimes be tricky. Throughout our relationship, we used to joke and laugh a lot. When she was dying, we talked about many of the things that used to make us laugh. We also talked about her dying. We even joked about it. Not that it was funny but that's the kind of person she was. When the end became obvious and I felt she knew it was obvious as well, I remember saying, "Go ahead. You know it's OK. You've had a good run." She looked at me right then…closed her eyes and died. I always thought she felt comfortable with me. I think she believed it was truly OK. I feel privileged to have been there.

My father died of a heart attack when he was in Florida. I was living in Texas at the time. I regret I never had the chance to say goodbye. He just went. That's a hard thing. It hurts more than anything. If I could relive a day or relive an experience, it would be his funeral. It was one of those where nobody knew what to do. It was horrible. The preacher was terrible. He didn't even know my father. Since that time, I have been to some beautiful funerals. My wife's mother and my wife's aunt had funerals that I thought were just beautiful, so sincere and so warm. You could feel the love. I wish I could give that to my father. My father was not sent away with the right spiritual dispatch. It hurts me that the real sense of him as a person did not come through at his funeral. I guess I feel it was truly a funeral and not a celebration of his life.

I believe when you die, if you are with someone you love and someone who loves you, it becomes a better experience for the dying person and for others, for closure for those left behind. You don't want to have not said something, not done something, not touched one more time. You don't want to feel that you have missed something.

I believe the energy, the spirit, the soul – whatever you want to call it – just lives on. I believe that the soul is around to help you if you need it. For example, my father died before my uncle – my mom's brother. My mother was quite distraught. She adored my father but she did what she had to do, she moved on as best she could. She was also quite close to my uncle. When my uncle died, my mother said that she wished Jack, her husband and my father, could be around to help him. I told her, "He is." I know he was there helping her to grieve. I did not say that to make her feel better. I said it because I felt my father's presence. I believe that if you are seeking that kind of help from someone that you really loved, you can reach out and they will be there.

Someone may have said something to you in your lifetime that sticks with you throughout your lifetime. They may have taught you a lesson. Somehow you get reminded of that lesson if it was significant enough. Who knows? You may wind up hearing a voice one day that brings the message back to you. There may be a physical thing that happens, like something landing on your shoulder and reminding you of something. It could be mental. It could be a physical hearing. I know a scientist might say thoughts are already in your subconscious and you're just retrieving them. All I know is that I strongly believe in angels. I believe there is something there. I believe there are angels who never lived on earth. I believe there are people who we loved on earth who died and came back in the form of an angel. One thing for sure, life goes on. It just takes on different forms.

This requires a lot of faith. Others say it might require a lot of naivety. Whatever the case, I think we'll all find out soon enough. The only thing I know is that I would hate to think that this human body is the only thing that I am. I would hate to think that all of the people I have loved, that their physical bodies represented all there is or was.

If I could craft the perfect day for the day after my death, I would probably try to find a way to contact my daughter. I have two daughters but one of them I believe would be more impacted than anyone else. I think she would be the most fragile. I would try to find a way to let her know that it's OK. I would tell her to go on living and do whatever she would want to do. She has always been my soul mate. I would try to make her not cry.

I don't want to die before I leave something behind but I am not afraid to die because I believe there is something else better afterwards. I might also throw reincarnation in here. We could come back as something else, maybe an animal. Maybe we'd come back as an angel and have the opportunity to touch someone else. We would have the chance to touch and guide and push someone else to a better life. I believe that can happen. What a beautiful thought.

Dying is a part of life. We should not be afraid of it. I totally believe there is a God and that God will take us in the right way. This is not the end of where we are. There is some sort of a resurrection. It's not a city paved in gold with honey dripping off the trees. Whatever life we live here…whatever mistakes we've make...whatever right or wrong, we're going to get another chance…somehow. Perfection is inside everybody, even those who do bad things. Perfection is trying to get out.

NISI

I think good people will go to heaven and bad people will go to hell. If you're good, you will go to a better place. Heaven is one big place where you are with God. My idea of heaven is sunflower fields and swings. I know that's where I would like to be. If your idea of heaven is swimming and doing things on the beach, that is what you'll be doing.

I would want my heaven to be sort of similar to how my life is now. I want it to be a place where all of my family is together. Since we all believe in God, we could all hang out together and have a great time. I'm sure you must believe in God to go to heaven.

Hell is something very much like where we are now but 10 times worse. It's like an earth with no God. People who don't care about other people, who don't believe in God, who don't lead decent lives go to hell. People who are mean at heart and who don't acknowledge the spiritual world go to hell.

If I died tonight, tomorrow I would probably be explaining to who ever is at the door, the things I did wrong and trying my best to get into heaven so I don't have to suffer an eternity. But if I am in heaven, I'm going to be spending time with my grandfather who I never got to meet. I will be talking to my grandmother who I was only with for a very short time, and all my other relatives that passed before me. I'll be talking and catching up and looking down on my other relatives who are still alive...and smiling.

I believe what I believe basically because I've been in Catholic school for 13 years. This just can't be all there is. There is too much pain and suffering and hatred and evil and just nastiness in this world for this to be it. This can't be it. After you die, something has to happen.

I have had experiences where relatives who have passed have come back to talk to me in my dreams. They are not in heaven; they are back down here. So I have never thought that once you die, you can't come back in some form or another.

For example, the night my cousin LaVar passed away from cancer, I was studying for a religion test before I went to sleep. I dreamed about him that night. He was alive at his home in Dayton. But in my dream, he had on a black hat, black boots, black shirt and a black jacket. He was sitting in like the TV room of his house. He had a lot of disfiguration from his cancer. In my dream, all of that was gone. He was speaking perfectly clearly. In life, he couldn't speak clearly because his voice and throat were affected by the cancer. He said, "Nisi, you stress too much and if you will just listen to me, you will know that you will be fine. You are going to graduate and be happy. You are going to go to the prom with who you want to go with and you will wear a beautiful dress. Everything will be fine. Your life will be OK. You don't need to worry." I don't know if I answered him or not. I was just sitting there. We were just talking. I think I might have nodded and said OK. I woke up and thought, "That's funny." I got dressed and then went into my parents' room to say goodbye like I did every other morning before school. They told me he died last night.

Another time, after he passed, I was coming into the house and, of course, I was stressing again and all of a sudden everything stopped. It was like the whole world

110

just stopped. I saw him and he told me, "Didn't I tell you that everything was going to be fine? Didn't I tell you that? Stop worrying." And he was right. Everything was fine. Everything I was worrying about turned out not to be a problem.

I'm not sure if I physically saw him standing before me but I did see him at least in my mind. More than once, as silly as it may seem, when relatives pass, at the moment that they pass, like with my cousin Alexis and with my Aunt Isaure, everything around me got silent. Everything around me goes quiet. Everything sort of dims for about two seconds. Then everything goes back to normal. I know that someone passed in my family. I don't know who but I know that someone passed. It's always been like that. I don't like funerals and coffins because it's a connection that reminds me of people I love who have gone. It scares me but that doesn't mean I don't want to hear from my relatives. So I pray to God every night that if my deceased relatives want to talk to me, let them talk to me. Even though I'm not sure if I see with my eyes or with my mind, I know that I do hear from my relatives. I always know when they visit.

When I see LaVar, I am going to tell him just how much we've missed him and how much things are not the same because he is not here with us. Going to Grandma's house is not the same. Eating Christmas dinner is not the same. Everything that we loved about Ohio died with him a little bit. I'm going to tell him how much of an impact he had on my life and on everyone else's life. He was so important.

I have learned that you need to take time to appreciate people. I remember times when LaVar teased me and I was so mad at him but I miss that now. I hope and pray for the day that we meet again but I also realize maybe I won't see him again.

111

So...What's Next?

So the lesson I've learned is while you have the time here on earth, you need to appreciate people and let them know how much they mean to you.

I believe that I am trying to live a decent life. I know there are a lot of things I do wrong but there are a lot of things I do right and if God decides that I'm worthy of going to heaven then yes, I believe we will meet again. I'm not John Edwards but I can feel things. I can kind of feel it when something's not right. I have some type of an awareness.

I'm going to be talking and laughing the day after I die. After I meet with all of my family, I will schedule an appointment with God because I have so much to ask Him.

ANGIE

If I died today, I would definitely be in Heaven with Jesus. I would be very happy. Nobody knows for sure what heaven is like but as a Christian you believe there is such a place. There are passages in the bible that tell you how to get to Heaven. You get there through Jesus Christ. There are some verses in Revelation about God's kingdom and no one knows if that's heaven or the millennium reign on earth when Jesus comes back. But it's like "streets of gold". A mansion is prepared for us. Just imagine its magnificence. There is no crying, no one is sick, no one is sad. The bible says there are no tears in heaven. No one promises no tears here on earth. Imagine that. No tears. No hardships. When you die, all of the suffering is gone…immediately!

I tend to think that the things that we think about here on earth, like houses and food and clothing, the things that we think about in terms of taking care of ourselves won't matter any more. I don't even know if there will be eating in heaven. I don't know how it's going to work but I know it's going to be great.

I think what I think because I am a Christian and I believe what the bible tells me as truth. They are God's words directly. I take that to heart. God is telling us how to live and how to be with Him in Heaven when we die. He says, "I am the way, the truth and the light." I believe that.

I know that everything in the bible is God breathed, God inspired. It's not just some historical compilation. The Bible is words that were given to people by God. God doesn't do that anymore. He doesn't have to because everything that He gives us in the bible is complete and whole and we don't need anything else. Can I prove it? No. It's faith. That's all I need.

For sure there are people who would do heinous things like bombing the World Trade Center not only in the name of someone but in the name of a so-called higher power. Well, we know that not to be correct. We know there were people like Hitler. I would assume he was not a Christian so he did not have Jesus Christ as his savior. That means Hitler is not going to Heaven. Something else we know is that there was a thief and a murderer on Jesus' sides when he was crucified. One was still mocking Him. The other believed in Him and recognized Jesus as the Lord. Jesus said to the sinner who believed that there was a place for him in Heaven. That sinner was promised salvation and that gives me faith that all of us who believe will also go to Heaven. The thing is, we are all sinners whether it be stealing or lying or jealousy or complaining. Much of the time we don't even know we are sinning. So it would be impossible to be saved if Jesus didn't help us.

I don't believe non-Christians go to Heaven. You get to Heaven because you have a personal relationship with Jesus. A friend of mine explained his thoughts to me. He said that Jesus existed but he was not the savior of the world. My friend will never get to Heaven because he does not have Jesus in his heart. If you don't ask Jesus into your heart, you are not going to get there. You cannot have a personal relationship with Jesus if you don't read the bible. You are not going to get into His kingdom.

I so strongly believe what I'm saying that I talk about it all the time. I want the people I care about to share eternity with me. I ask the Holy Spirit to help me help them. The Holy Spirit has to lead you to accept. There is nothing I can say or do to change a person's mind. There is no magic formula. If there was, everyone would be writing it down and making sure that all of their loved ones would be saved. Nobody wants someone they love to be banished to hell. Eternity is forever. If you think things are bad here on earth, don't wind up in hell!

These are some fun thoughts but I believe in them. I will be able to eat a ton of stuff in Heaven and I won't gain weight. I will be able to fly. I will ask God a bunch of questions about things. During our lifetime, we go through so many things we just don't understand. We don't really know the purpose of anything. Life is difficult at best. We don't understand things that don't directly happen to us. Still, they are things that affect and disturb us. We just don't understand. I plan to ask God, "What were you thinking about?" Think about certain animals, like a giraffe. I'd ask God how he came up with that one. I think I would just be happy to be there and learn all kinds of things.

There is no doubt in my mind. There is a heaven and a hell. I like to know details and specifics. I like facts and data but I can't get any specifics about heaven. It's all about faith. Faith is belief in something you cannot see, feel and touch. I had faith when I sat down in this chair, it would hold me up.

I know God is not going to let me down. There are situations that have happened in my life that I don't like. There are some awful things that have happened but believe it or not, those things happened for my good. I think bad things make us better people. We learn and we grow from adversity.

Everyone has their own idea of what heaven is, what it's like and how to get there. But until one realizes that we are all sinners and that we have to turn away from sin and towards Jesus and ask Him into our hearts, we'll never get there. I firmly believe this. I believe it true for all people. My thought is obviously not a popular thought with everyone but it is my total belief. It's not that I don't like other people or other religions. I just believe Christianity is the only way. You can believe what you want but if it's not about Jesus, you're wrong.

It's very comforting to think, "What is the worst thing that could happen to me?" Well, someone would kill me. That would certainly be bad. I would not be happy but I know that immediately I would be in heaven and I wouldn't even think about it anymore. So how bad is it really? Jesus is waiting for me.

ALTA

Just about all of what I believe is based on the deaths of my loved ones - primarily my brother and father. Maybe because they are the most recent. Maybe because they were the most unexpected. I think about them together. Not one at a time. So when I talk about them, I mix their stories and remembrances together.

My triplet brother Alexis died very young. I feel like he should still be living. I feel like there was so much more that he could have done. He did not have a chance to experience so many things. I realize that the body was not meant to live forever but I also believe love *is* forever. What I feel more than anything is the love between Alexis and me. My mother still lives in the house we all grew up in. I have four other siblings. When I go home, I go into Alexis' room. I feel his love. I feel his presence.

Last night, I went into the backyard to talk to my brother and also to talk to so many other relatives who have died. While I was out there just kind of running around and going with my intuition, following my heart and dancing back and forth, all of a sudden this cool breeze just sort of kicked in. And it just sort of blew me from side to side for about 2 or 3 minutes. I truly felt that it was a sign from the spirits, especially my brother, my father and my grandmother who lived with us in this house. It was a sign that let me know that they were listening…and that they knew I was trying to communicate with them. I was really just thanking them for loving me and giving me life. I think they were giving me a kiss back…in the form of a breeze that came from nowhere.

At the moment I felt the breeze, I believed it was a message. It is comforting to me to believe in messages. I think that was one. I have had other messages that I believe came from my father. There are some things that stand out in my mind. They are things that happened after my father passed. Strange things were happening in our house. Lights were burning out. Lights were flickering. The stove would stop working and then all of a sudden, start working again. The doorbell stopped working. There were a lot of electrical things going on in the house that were out of the ordinary. I have read that that's how spirits let others know they are around. These things had not normally happened previous to his death. That's why I attribute them *to* his death.

I remember one time I was driving my father's car. It was about a week after he died. This was the very first time I had driven his Jeep. He loved his Jeep and he didn't want anyone driving it. Anyway, I got in and turned on the radio. The song "Father Figure" was playing. Could that possibly be a coincidence? Maybe so. Maybe not. But this is how I interpreted it. It was a message from my father. He was saying, "I was your father figure. I am still here. I still love you." Why would that particular song be on at that particular time? The song was years old at that time. I was sitting in my father's car, in his seat...something I had wanted to do for a long time...something I had been waiting to do for a long time. I find that more than coincidence.

Something else significant happened that I would like to tell you about. A bunch of trash piled up in front of the house. It was at the time that Alexis, my brother, passed. There were a lot of people at our house after the service. The trash had not been picked up and a bunch of dogs got into it. It was strewn all over the front yard. My mother asked me to go outside and clean it up. I remember it was really wet and muddy and messy. No one wanted the job but it fell on my shoulders. So I went outside with rubber gloves on and I proceeded to pick up every piece of wet paper, trash and food. I put everything into the trash bag. I remember even having to use a shovel. Remember this was after my brother's service so there was just an extraordinary amount of food in the trash. It seems like everything was gross and molded. It was also near a holiday so there was a lot of paper from gifts. Anyway, I remember when I got to the bottom of the pile, there was a photograph. It was in perfect condition. It wasn't wet. It wasn't damaged in any way at all. It was a photograph of my father. The date on it was 1962. The funny thing is he was the same age on the photograph that I was on the day that I found it. I just thought that was really strange. It was a message to me that he appreciated what I had done.

I remember also during that time, I would seem to notice my father's initials. No place in particular…I would just seem to often see "J.L.". They would just seem to stand out…like on license plates and signs. That was sort of a strange happening that impressed me for some reason.

I also had problems for a while in my own apartment in Brooklyn. The lights in my living room would flicker. The television would turn on and off all by itself. I finally got angry and said, "Would you please stop? This is frightening me." And the flickering stopped. Who knows? Maybe it's not related at all but I am convinced it is. These events usually occur around the time something else significant is happening in my life. For example, I have a bird clock in my kitchen. The bird sings on the hour. Well, for some reason, the bird stopped singing a while back. The clock still works but the bird won't sing. I've tried to fix it but I can't seem to. But every now and then, the bird sings a little and it's when something great is going on in my life…or when I'm feeling unusually upbeat, it sings. I attribute the bird's sporadic singing as a sign from my father saying, " I'm so happy for you." I really believe that. I can't see any other reason why, say, once a month or once every two months, the songs just start playing. Another thing, if I oversleep, the singing starts and it wakes me up. I can be in a deep sleep and all of a sudden, the singing starts.

My sister Kitty tells me that she dreams about a cousin of ours who died. She says Mayumi came to her. She didn't say anything. She just came to her. I have heard that not to be an uncommon experience. Spirits come to you and they don't talk. The reason is that they don't want to frighten you. They're really not trying to communicate with you verbally. Their objective is to communicate with you spiritually through thoughts. Anyway, Mayumi has visited my sister several times...six or seven. I know that Mayumi felt close to Kitty and her husband. She spent a lot of time with them.

Mayumi was quite heavy most of her life. But in Kitty's dream, Mayumi was thin and very gorgeous. I think I understand that. I believe we take the form where we felt the best during our lifetimes – in whatever shape or form or size that would have been.

Many of my relatives have come to me in dreams. The first time my father came to me, I was at my apartment in Brooklyn. I remember I was really sad that day. I remember I cried half that day. I couldn't move on that day. I was stuck...thinking about him. I called my mother and talked to her about my sadness and loneliness. When I went to bed that night, he came to me in a dream. He told me that I was going to be OK. In the dream, we were sitting on a couch together. He told me that he was really happy I had left Ray, my cat, in Detroit with my mother because, he said, she needs the company. It was a pleasant dream. Most of them are pleasant.

My brother has come to me a handful of times. This one time really stands out because I really thought he was in the room with me. I felt like I saw a vision when I woke up. When he came to me, there was a red glow around his face. It was like a halo with very vivid colors. It was at a time when I was in Brooklyn feeling sort of isolated and alone and sad because I missed him a lot. He came to me to tell me that everything was going to work out. While he didn't say anything, that was the thought that was put in my mind. I heard his voice in my mind. But his lips did not move. He hovered above my bed. And when I woke up, I felt like I was on top of the world. It lifted my spirits. I felt better. I was so happy I jumped out of the bed.

I would like for them to visit me more often. My sister says they come to her and she doesn't even think about it or ask for it. I think for some reason, they must find it easy to come to her. It must be because she's so healthy and care free. She doesn't seem to have a lot of stress in her life. That could make it easy to approach her. When our brother first passed, Kitty was afraid because he used to come to her all the time. I wish I were as "reachable".

I had a premonition before my father passed. It was actually about four years before he passed. I saw him in an ambulance. The way he really did die was the way it happened in my dream. I remember him being in the ambulance and being told that he had a heart attack. It was something that happened very quickly. It was one of the few times I actually cried while dreaming. I woke up and my pillow was wet and my face was covered with tears. I called my father immediately just to make sure he was OK. And he was. I didn't take it to mean anything at all. I just figured I had a bad dream. But now I believe it was a premonition. I wish I had thought of that at the time. Maybe I would have spent more time with him. Although I am comfortable with the time I spent with him, in hindsight, you always wish you had done better.

A few days after Alexis died, I was sleeping with my mother and I was sleeping on my father's side of the bed. I had a very vivid dream of Alexis and my father on a shuttle bus. I saw their faces through the window. They waved at me and the bus kept going. It was a short dream but it was warm. It was a very bright day in the dream. I could feel the sun as the bus was driving past me. It made me feel good. The dream told me that they are together. That was the message. I found it very comforting. I have become interested in the whole process of grieving. I wonder what it really means. I wonder if it ever really ends.

This is what I envision if I died tonight. Tomorrow, I would explore and become familiar with my new environment. It would be very luscious. There would be lots of trees and mountains...flowers and grass. There would be beautiful buildings. Perceptions would be so much more emotional than physical. I would use all of the lessons I learned in the physical world...those that made me a better person. I would be able to treat other spirits better because I would be a better soul. I would have higher standards...because I believe in a higher power. God is in all of us. God is in every little thing.

I think I would be celebrating with my ancestors. But I'm not exactly sure that all of my ancestors would be there because THEY had ancestors before them. So I think that different groups come together, the groups that maybe were the closest to each other or spent the most time together on earth. My father would probably meet me first and help me through the transition. Then he would take me to where all of my other ancestors are. I believe that the form we take in the spiritual world is a form where we probably were at our best during our life on earth.

I think God is using my father. I think he did a lot of great things. He helped people. He worked with hospice. I think he probably came to the point where he could be an instrument for God. I think my father evolved a tremendous amount during his lifetime so his last lifetime might in fact be the last. God needed him so He took him. He will use him in some way because my father came so far...a loving kind human being...a caretaker.

My brother, I think he will come back again because he never realized self-actualization. He was challenged and maybe never learned the lessons he should have. He left too soon. He may have already returned...not as he was when he was here before. Not the same. Not totally different. Some of his soul might be back in another soul.

LISE PAULINE

I believe that somewhere down the line, we all get reincarnated. We all have this feeling of having been somewhere before but we know we have probably never stepped foot in that place before. We look at someone and think, "I know this person" but we've probably never met them.

The whole concept of dying is really freaky to me. It's the concept of lying there still...for eternity. I'm not one to sit still for a long period of time. So I figure there has to be some place. There is a heaven. You go there and you become this other person. You get reincarnated. You become either an animal or another person. I think whatever happens to you in this life has something to do with what happens to you in the next life. I think most of us will come back as human beings. It's that weird phenomenon where you find people reflecting back in thought and feeling.

I believe people come back as different people...even allowing ourselves a chance to do things differently than we may have done in a previous life. Of course none of us are conscious of the fact that we died (if, in fact, we did) and came back from it. So, we don't really know what happens but I believe we get a second chance. Who is to say we haven't lived since (say) the 1500s? Maybe we have lived multiple lives. A cat has nine lives. Why can't we have nine? I can see myself living in the 1500s in medieval times when we didn't have the things that we have now. Maybe the things I went through then, I can change now and do things a whole lot differently. People are people. Times change but people go through the same things...job security...whatever. Maybe I was poor but in the next lifetime, I become a millionaire. The only problem is: I wouldn't remember it.

If I died tonight, tomorrow I think I would be golfing. If I could be doing anything tomorrow, I would simply live that day to the fullest. I would be so happy to have the second chance to do something else. We take for granted that everything is always here for us. It's sad that I could leave here today and get hit by a car and there are tons of things that I have not yet been able to do. I haven't been married. I don't have kids. I have not yet lived the full life that I want to live. I try to live every day to the fullest. I might not have a great job and I might not have things other people have (that security) but I do the things I like. I travel. I have fun and I'm living the life that I want to live right now. And I can always say, I did the things I want to do...as much as I could, before I die. So, I'm hoping that if I get that second chance, I can just continue doing the things and living the life I want to live.

I can't wait until I go to heaven and spend time with my grandfather and my grandmother. I never really knew my grandfather. For me, that would be the ultimate. I hear he was a great guy. He loved to have fun. I can just see him and my grandmother. We're just playing cards and having a good time. I think what I look forward to now, even as a young person (my mom always says I'm such an old soul), I love listening to the things of the past...how "they" used to do things. I wasn't there. Obviously, I never got to see that. I would really like to be able to spend time with loved ones and talk with them about what "they" were going through growing up. I would love to hear about the things they did because they achieved some major accomplishments in life...and from little means.

I would also love to talk to some people like William Shakespeare. But if there is anyone I could connect with, it would definitely be my family. There is so much I would love to learn especially from the relatives I really never knew like great-

great grandparents. Until we accept and learn our past, we can't go forward. It would be great to go back even farther to people who had already crossed over before I was born.

What form do I see that taking? I literally can see us around the table playing cards, talking. My grandmother and I used to do that when I was little. We'd have great conversations. They may have been about nothing but I loved it. I remember when my grandmother passed, I thought that she was probably in heaven with a drink in one hand and a cigarette in the other having a good time. I mean – back in her element. My grandfather is right next to her. At one point, you can even get a little envious because you say, " I kind of want to be there too." It's not that I want to die tomorrow but I just would like not to have to deal with pain and suffering... things here that are not there. It's an oasis of happiness and tranquility.

Not everyone will go in the direction of heaven. I do believe there is also a hell and a purgatory somewhere in the middle. I don't know if heaven is pearly white gates and clouds. I do believe it is a place for peoples' souls to go when they die, a place to be with loved ones who died before them. I would call it a country club or a resort, a place to be around people you love. It's a place where you are free from sickness and disease and violence and all of the unpleasant things we deal with here.

If you had to determine who goes to heaven and who goes to hell, how would you do that? Suppose you've been a good person, a model citizen...you've done everything right...OK, you can go to heaven. What if the next person stole a car and maybe did some other things but you could have been a good person at heart. You just chose the wrong path. Does that necessarily mean that they have to go to hell? It's pretty touchy. I can see if you're a convicted person and you've killed thousands of people and you have no remorse…then you should go to hell. But I wonder what happens to those people who did some things wrong but deep down inside, they were still good people. Maybe they took good care of their children but maybe they had to be a prostitute to do that. There are so many circumstances out there. It's hard to determine who goes where. I guess I'm saying I don't want to determine that. That must be what purgatory is for…to see if you'll make it to heaven. Maybe it's a place for souls that have not found peace.

I believe there are hauntings. There are people whose souls have not rested. They are stuck. They are trying to find a place for themselves. I used to feel like my grandfather was like that…always around. I believe he was telling me, "I'm always here for you." The lights used to flicker in my apartment for no apparent reason. The stereo would come on for no apparent reason. Of course at first it freaks you out but then I realized it was him. He was letting me know again that he is here for me.

The reason I think it's him is because of something that happened to me when my family lived in Pittsburgh. I was in the kitchen and the babysitter was in the living room which was quite a distance from the kitchen. I felt a heavy hand press upon my shoulder. I turned around and no one was there. I was about 11 or 12 at the time. I didn't really think anything too much at first. So I went on about my business and then I felt the hand again. I got scared then and thought maybe the babysitter was playing a joke on me. But there would not have been enough time for her to run back without me seeing her. It was kind of freaky but it was also a comforting thing. The only thing I really remember about my grandfather is that he used to hold me a lot. He had heavy hands. Even though I was only one, I remember his hands. I just kind of knew that was him because of the hands.

All of this kind of makes me wonder if I have some kind of a connection with the other side. It doesn't bother me at all. I have spoken with other people who feel the same way. They believe they can feel the presence of someone gone. It makes sense to me. I believe it's a matter of protection. It becomes a comfort. They make you feel like, "I'm here."

Another thing, I have dreamed about something specific like standing in a specific spot in the kitchen with a couple of specific people there...talking about something very specific. It's a dream. But then years later, that specific incident becomes reality. It happened exactly as I dreamed it years before. It happens all the time. It's like foreseeing something.

I was in an automobile accident a couple of years ago. I was in the car with my best friend running errands for her wedding. It didn't dawn on me at the time of the accident but after I had some time to regroup...I realized how familiar the scene was. Everything that happened, step by step, everything that I said to her in a dream years earlier, I said to her in the car...after the accident.

I saw my life flash before my eyes. Everything went white. I didn't realize it immediately but the airbags had deployed. But I did see bits and snippets. I saw my parents. I saw my brother. I saw special occasions. I saw a trip. It was really weird. It's not like a slow motion thing where you see your whole life like from the time you were a kid...like in the movies and they just start fast-forwarding. I had quick visions of things that meant the most to me. Christmas dinner is special to me. I saw Christmas dinner with my whole family.

My next thought was of my friend. I began to bargain with God. I told God that if He had to take one of us make it me because this was my girlfriends wedding. I wanted her to be able to have her wedding. I didn't want to die but she was my best friend and I wanted her to have her day. My girlfriend started screaming all of a sudden and that's when things came back into focus. I guess God didn't want either of us.

I need to be at peace with myself when I die. If you are not at peace, your soul cannot rest. I have told my mother what I want when I die, who I want to carry my casket, what songs I want sung. I want everybody to have a party. Have a good time. I don't want my grieving parents to have to worry about details. I will take care of them myself.

The hard part of it for me is just lying there...never being able to move again. That's what bothers me the most. I cannot even lie in my bed for long periods of time. It freaks me out. I hate lying still. The thought of never being able to move again is just weird. Even when I go to funerals, I look at bodies and I think to myself...I wonder if they're just going to jump up. Maybe I don't accept death.

All I know is that I don't want to look back and wish I had done things. I don't want to look down from heaven and say I had not lived my life to the fullest. I don't want to regret anything.

JIMMY

I have a certain amount of prejudice because I was raised in a church-going, golden rule sort of a family. I even attended a seminary. I got involved in fundamental religion but I have backed away from that and have gotten involved in a more traditional or mainstream type of religion. Traditional religion teaches us that there is a better life. There is a paradise of some sort. You don't know what form that takes until you get there. But you often wonder about what happens after you die. Does anything happen to my body? I doubt it. Does it happen to my soul? Probably! But who can be sure until you cross that line.

I have often reflected on the idea that human beings are the only living creatures who know they are going to die. Human beings, if it's a matter of evolution, have actually come to the place where there is so much going on with them and they are able to accomplish so much for the good of each other and for themselves, it would seem like such a terrible waste if something didn't live on. It's just like if you're created to be an intellectual, to be a leader or something like that, it would be such a terrible waste for that life to cease to exist.

On the other hand, you can mix that up with a sense of arrogance and that would be wrong, too. I'm fond of a saying that at the end of a game, the king and the pawns are put away in the same box. So if you find yourself kind of worshipping people who are big leaders in the world or celebrities in some way, you should be careful not to be in too much awe of them. All of us are leaders in some way.

When I was a child, and a product of teachers and mentors and the like, they were teaching us…be a good boy and you go to Heaven, the streets are paved with gold and that sort of thing. I don't want to step on anybody's toes but if you believe literally what you read in scriptures about that, my hat is off to you. I'm not sure that I do 100% but I kind of lean towards it. I believe it's got some sort of basis in truth or reality or whatever you want to call it but it's also a visual. It is something we can recognize, maybe understand, maybe accept.

There is a constant fight between the emotional/spiritual man and the intellectual man. For the intellectual man the prevailing thought is when you die, you're dead and that's it. You were here...you're gone...period. I'm not sure I really think that's the case. On the other hand, I think it's wrong for people to just keep building their lives in such a way that nobody will ever forget them no matter what. Some people really live to do that...to create such an aura and mystery about themselves that no one will ever forget them. Maybe it's not so important people remember me 100 years from now. There are countless numbers of great people who came before me...famous and not so famous. Do I remember them? Not necessarily.

I have never actually felt the presence of a loved one who passed away. But we are products of our upbringing and I find myself asking myself, "What would Dad do in a case like this?" So in that sense there is a presence, but it was a presence that took place a long time ago and imprinted itself on me. I tend to react like he would because of my love for him. I feel much the same about my mother. I was very close to my Dad. I just saw in his memorial service how many people came not only to pay their respects but to tell me how much they loved my dad. They didn't have to do that but it's obvious my dad made an impression on them as he made on me.

If I died today, what would I be doing tomorrow? Who knows? I wish I could say with great certainty. I guess if nothing else, I'm proving I'm very ambiguous in my thoughts about it. I really don't know. I would like to think that some part of me would be able to hover around and see how things turn out. On the other hand, is that really important? I don't know. When you're gone you're gone. You can't take anything with you. We've all heard that. Emotion and love and things like that seemingly would have to be broken away by being dead, by being gone. You know you live on in the hearts of people close to you for a while but even time changes that. It should because life is for the living.

I tend to have as my closest friends those who are most like my dad in their values, what they consider to be important, in their sense of honesty, fairness and things like that. I admired my dad so I think I subconsciously look for those traits in other people. It makes me comfortable to be around people with traits I admire. I trust them with my inner most secrets. It shows the difference in a close friend and an acquaintance.

I also believe that's my father's spirit living on. That, to me, is living on. So maybe that's the definition of paradise in a way. It's the legacy you leave by the way that you lived your life. So the people who knew you the best and admired some of your traits enough to adopt those traits in their own lives...continue to keep the chains linked from generation to generation. Maybe that's why evil doesn't really succeed over good in the long run because there is always good being created and being remembered, valued and passed along to generations ahead.

Evil is also being created (pedophilia, violent crimes, cheap life, murders, drive by shootings). I try to put my self in the place of the person who committed what

I consider to be a heinous crime and I think, "What dark thing in me would ever make me cross the line?" I have come to the conclusion that I never would cross that line. So what's the difference? I'm not sure I can define it but I think somehow or another the lack of training or value in their lives, which they maybe had no control over, caused evil to rise up. I don't mean this arrogantly but I don't think I would ever do horribly evil things. I see the dignity of human beings. I love it.

I wish I could sit and talk with great certainty. I cannot. But I do know that my creator does not fear intellectual inquisitiveness. I believe that however I came to be on this earth, my questioning is wanted and cherished in its own way because I have been given a capacity to question. There is nothing wrong with that. There is no blind following. There are always questions. There is importance to life and how you live it. I am hoping for the best. We don't have the option of saying, "Hey I'm out of here in x number of years." We need a goal. We can't be evil. If you don't believe there is a here after, you don't have motivation to do the right thing. For all of us, I believe we know the right thing even if we don't live it. We may not come to any conclusions but it's important to talk about it. Man has dominion over lesser creatures.

Have you ever heard the story about God and a scientist having a discussion? The scientist says to God, "You know, these days, we really don't need You. I mean, just think about it. With cloning and the like, we can even create human beings. We can do what You can do." God says "Go ahead. Let me see." The scientist reaches down and picks up a hand of dirt. God stops him and says, 'Wait a minute. Use your own dirt."

It's fun talking about this. It's a challenge. Why would one species rise above all the others? Why would one species ask questions about how one lives and thinks and feels and acts? What would be the point of living and trying to make life better for it to be (snap) all over? It just doesn't make sense.

MY PARTY...THE LAST CHAPTER!

There are as many opinions as to what happens after this life on this earth as there are people on this earth. We all have our own very personal ideas fueled by our own very personal reasons.

I have often thought as I look back on my life, that if I could construct what might be next, I would pick maybe ten weeks worth of the best days of my life and I would live those days over and over again. Of course they would be days filled with happiness and laughter. They would be days when no one is sick and worries are nonexistent. They would be days when I was a child but somehow, my children and my husband would be there also. There would be beautiful, funny, silly, carefree days in Detroit, in Nashville as well as spotty vacation days around the country and the world. My eternally re-lived days would be those I felt significant and worthwhile...days I loved and felt loved. They would be days I learned something and passed it on. They would be days that something happened or days I met someone who made me glad I was me.

This is a perfect example explaining what I mean. Through my twenty-five year career in television, I had the opportunity to meet several well-known and accomplished people. I learned that celebrity comes for many reasons and in various packages. Celebrities are not always athletes, rock stars or entertainers. Of the countless number of "famous" people I had the opportunity of meeting and interviewing, I was most impressed with Osceola McCarty.

You may remember that she was the African American woman from Hattiesburg, Mississippi. She never had the opportunity of a college education. In fact, she had a third grade education. She dropped out of school at about 8 years old to help take care of an ailing aunt. She learned throughout her life that her lack of an education held her back. She was, in fact, a washer woman who washed and ironed loads of other people's clothes for sometimes as little as 50 cents a bundle. She lived in a little tiny house, never had a car and not until close to the end of her life, did she have a little black and white television. At any rate, through her life's work, she was able to save a substantial amount of money and she donated most of it to the University of Mississippi for scholarship opportunities for African American students. If I remember correctly, it was about $150,000, donated for higher education from a WASHER WOMAN!

God bless Osceola McCarty! I had the privilege of acting as Mistress of Ceremonies at a Sojourner Truth Foundation Dinner in Detroit one evening and Ms. McCarty was the special guest. I felt as though I was in the presence of true greatness. I was aware of her before I accepted the emcee position. She is why I accepted it. When I met her I was so humbled, it brought me to tears.

Why am I telling you this? Because one of my ten weeks worth of days in heaven would be with Osceola McCarty. I'd love to talk with her some more. I'd like to look into her face and tell her what a beautiful person she was and how I thought her act of selflessness taught stupid, educated me what life is all about. She was very aware of not having an education but I want to be sure she knows that an uneducated African American woman from the south taught the world something the books could never have touched.

And so as I continue to think about what's next...if I died tonight, what would I be doing tomorrow, as I have asked all interviewed for this book, I would invite

Osceola to my party, the one I'm going to have after God checks me in. I hope she likes Papa John's pizza and Diet Coke because that's what I'm going to serve. By the way, I'll be drinking Diet Coke because I like it. Not because I'll be on a diet. My mother and father and brother and all of my beautiful family and friends will be there. We are going to eat and drink and smoke. We are not going to gain weight or get sick because you will be allowed to do whatever you want. The food won't make you fat and the cigarettes won't give you cancer. We are going to talk and laugh and before you know it, it's a century later!

Printed in the United States
71055LV00009B/125